DEVONSHIRE
CHRISTMAS

A
DEVONSHIRE
CHRISTMAS

MIKE HOLGATE

For my granddaughter Amelie's first Christmas

First published 2009

The History Press
The Mill, Brimscombe Port
Stroud, Gloucestershire, GL5 2QG
www.thehistorypress.co.uk

British Library Cataloguing in Publication Data.
A catalogue record for this book is available from the British Library.

ISBN 978 0 7524 5170 1

Typesetting and origination by The History Press
Printed in Great Britain

CONTENTS

THE AUTHOR

Mike Holgate lives in Torquay and has worked as a writer, musician and librarian since obtaining an honours degree from Plymouth University in 1988. The author of several books, he is a regular contributor to *Devon Life* magazine and his research on one of the contributors featured in this book, John 'Babbacombe' Lee, was used by Granada Television for the crime series *In Suspicious Circumstances* in 1995, and a BBC Radio Devon play *A Shadow of Doubt – the Story of The Man They Couldn't Hang* in 2008.

ACKNOWLEDGEMENTS

The author would like to express his gratitude for access to the archives and resources available from his employer, Torbay Library Services. Extracts have been taken from the impressive range of antiquarian books available at the John Pike Local Studies Room at Torquay Library, while images have been obtained from the Local Studies Illustration file at Torquay Reference Library and the following illustrated newspapers and antiquarian books: *Illustrated London News*, *Illustrated Police News*, *Punch*, *Torquay Times*, *John Leech's Pictures of Life and Character* and William Phillip's *Carols: Their Origin, Music and Connection with Mystery Plays*.

INTRODUCTION

Charles Dickens described Devon as 'the most beautiful of counties' when he brought his family to live in Exeter. The author, who began the tradition of the seasonal ghost story with the classic *A Christmas Carol*, is one of several famous residents whose works are featured in this varied collection of carols, songs, poems, mysteries, folklore and memories. Alongside extracts from the works of writers including Charles Kingsley, Eden Phillpotts, Sabine Baring-Gould, Beatrice Chase, Anna Eliza Bray, Robert Herrick and Henry Francis Lyte are a collection of my own seasonal essays about the lives and experiences of famous personalities including Agatha Christie, Rudyard Kipling, Henry Williamson, Lady Nancy Astor, Isambard Kingdom Brunel and Oscar Wilde.

On Christmas Eve, the ancient tradition of 'wassailing' in apple orchards ensures the successful production of the county's favourite tipple – 'Demsur' cider. The festive season is strongly associated with celebratory drinking and ghostly tales, therefore the stories within illustrate how the two themes are often interlinked. Bouts of drinking often lead to the telling of tall tales, and drunks wandering through churchyards either believe they have seen an apparition or have been mistaken for ghosts themselves.

With apologies to Cliff Richard for the corruption of the title of one of his most popular Christmas No. 1's, there is a section of true crime stories with a seasonal twist entitled 'Christmas Time – Mystery and Crime' including classic tales of the failed execution of condemned murderer John Lee, the police hunt for the missing crime novelist Agatha Christie, and a seasonal performance by an actor later identified as Jack the Ripper.

In our neighbouring county across the River Tamar, the natives have a reputation for baking anything edible. So much so, it is said, that 'The Devil will not come into Cornwall for fear of being put in a pie'. His Satanic Majesty has no such fear of Devon and practices his own peculiar culinary skills preparing 'soul' food on Dartmoor at the Devil's Kitchen, the Devil's Frying Pan and the Devil's Punchbowl. Demonic 'hot tips' utilising the 'evils of drink' accompany the seasonal dishes recommended by the original 'domestic goddess', Mrs Beeton. These recipes reflect the old adage that 'God sends food, but the Devil sends cooks!'

May God bless you and the Devil miss you

A very merry Christmas and a happy New Year!

Mike Holgate
Torquay 2009

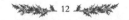

one

THE SPIRIT OF CHRISTMAS PAST

CHRISTMAS CRACKERS |

Why is a plum cake like an ocean?
Because it contains many currants.

Exeter Flying Post, 24 December 1913

Dickens in Devon

To Victorian England, the nation's favourite novelist, Charles Dickens, embodied the spirit of Christmas. His many seasonal works included the classic story *A Christmas Carol* which was published in the same decade that saw the introduction of the Christmas card, the Christmas cracker and the Christmas tree.

Dickens provided his parents with a home near Exeter and based many of his literary characters on people he observed in the area. With the help of wealthy social reformer Baroness Angela Burdett-Coutts he fought the twin evils of 'Ignorance' and 'Want', revealed by the Ghost of Christmas Present in the author's heart-warming parable *A Christmas Carol*. In the story Scrooge, a miserable old skinflint, is shown the error of his ways by three ghosts who teach him the true spirit of Christmas and its essential Christian element of 'goodwill to all men'. Written in 1843, Charles Dicken's literary masterpiece exposed the hypocrisy of the 'Victorian Christmas', using the festive season as a backdrop to highlight social injustice. Like many of his novels, the story carried a moral which pricked the conscience of the rich and helped to change society's attitude to the plight of the poor. Victorian indifference to the impoverished was memorably illustrated by Scrooge's response when asked for a charitable donation to provide families with some Christmas cheer, 'Are there no prisons? No workhouses for these people?' At the age of twelve Dickens was working in a shoe-blacking warehouse while the rest of his family were imprisoned and held responsible for debts incurred by his father. Kind-hearted dreamer John Dickens provided the inspiration for the character of Wilkins Micawber; always 'expecting something to turn up' in the semi-autobiographical *David Copperfield*. Dickens bailed his father out of debtors' prison on four occasions before moving his parents out of reach of their London creditors to live in Devon at Mile End Cottage, Alphington. Here he wrote several chapters of *Nicholas Nickleby*.

Dickens practised what he preached and was a generous benefactor. His leading disciple was Baroness Angela Burdett-Coutts. He dedicated *Martin Chuzzlewit* to her and described the wealthy heiress as his 'soul-mate'. For twenty years she made her home in Torquay. Her con-

Charles Dickens.

tributions to charitable causes are incalculable. She was a founder member of the NSPCC and provided thousands of children with 'hot meals for a penny'. Agreeing with Dickens' assertion that anyone could be improved by 'education and example', she set up free reading rooms and night school institutions all over the country. Her financial backing established a home for reforming London prostitutes and Dickens personally visited prisons to plead the case of young girls to be released to their care.

Dickens and the baroness both had idiosyncratic love lives. Charles openly admitted to his 'unhealthy fixation' with Queen Victoria and was inconsolable when she married Prince Albert. He took a wife who bore a striking resemblance to the Queen. The couple had ten children before separating when she discovered he was having affairs with her sister and a young actress. The youthful Angela Burdett-Coutts had wanted to marry the Duke of Wellington, forty-five years her senior. Then, in old age, she scandalised society by announcing her betrothal to an American forty years her junior. When Queen Victoria heard of this unlikely union she remarked that the baroness was 'a silly old woman'. Despite the doubters, the marriage survived happily for twenty-six years until the philanthropist fell ill one Christmas and succumbed at the age of ninety-two. In recognition of her life's work for charitable causes she was buried in Westminster Abbey in the nave, near the west door, in 1907.

Charles Dickens aged prematurely and at the age of fifty-seven announced a 'farewell tour' of readings from his works. He had described his first appearance in Devon at Exeter as 'the finest audience I ever read to'. His final appearance in the county attracted a large crowd at Torquay in January 1869. The *Torquay Directory* reported that people travelled from as far as Plymouth and Exeter and had trouble getting home as 'the police had a very difficult task in keeping order, and to direct the arrangement of the carriages'. England's greatest Victorian writer died the following year. To commemorate the centenary of his death, a plaque was donated by Edith Wheeler of the Newton Abbot Writers circle and unveiled at Mile End Cottage by distinguished Devon author R.F. Delderfield on 9 June 1970. The official party then attended a reception in Exeter at the Turks Head, a favourite haunt of Dickens. No doubt the toast was Tiny Tim's wish for mankind, 'God bless us, every one!'

A Christmas Carol

Charles Dickens composed this carol, sung by Mr Wardle in *The Pickwick Papers* (1837):

I care not for Spring; on his fickle wing
Let the blossoms and buds be borne;
He woos them amain with his treacherous rain,
And he scatters them ere the morn.
An inconstant elf, he knows not himself,
Nor his own changing mind an hour,
He'll smile in your face, and, with witty grimace,
He'll wither your youngest flower.

Let the Summer sun to his bright home run,
He shall never be sought by me;
When he's dimmed by a cloud I can laugh aloud
And care not how sulky he be!
For his darling child is the madness wild
That sports in fierce fever's train;
And when love is too strong, it don't last long,
As many have found to their pain.

A mild harvest night, by the tranquil light
Of the modest and gentle moon,
Has a far sweeter sheen to me, I ween,
Than the broad and unblushing noon.
But every leaf awakens my grief,
As it lieth beneath the tree;
So let Autumn air be never so fair,
It by no means agrees with me.

But my song I troll out, for Christmas stout,
The hearty, the true, and the bold;
A bumper I drain, and with might and main
Give three cheers for this Christmas old!
We'll usher him in with a merry din
That shall gladden his joyous heart,
And we'll keep him up, while there's bite or sup,
And in fellowship good, we'll part.

In his fine honest pride, he scorns to hide
One jot of his hard-weather scars;
They're no disgrace, for there's much the same trace

On the cheeks of our bravest tars.
Then again I sing till the roof doth ring
And it echoes from wall to wall -
To the stout old wight, fair welcome to-night,
As the King of Seasons all!

Christmas Day

By Charles Kingsley from *Poems* (1897). Born at Holne
Vicarage, the eminent author whose classic novel *Westward
Ho!* inspired the birth of a seaside resort, produced this sea-
sonal ode in 1868:

How will it dawn, the coming of Christmas Day?
A northern Christmas, such as painters love,
And kinsfolk, shaking hands but once a year,
And dames who tell old legends by the fire?
Red sun, blue sky, white snow, and pearled ice,
Keen ringing air, which sets the blood on fire,
And makes the old man merry with the young,
Through the short sunshine, through the longer night?

Or southern Christmas, dark and dank with mist,
And heavy with the scent of steaming leaves,
And rosebuds mouldering on the dripping porch;
One twilight, without rise or set of sun,
Till beetles drone along the hollow lane,
And round the leafless hawthorns, flitting bats
Hawk the pale moths of winter? Welcome then

Charles Kingsley.

At best, the flying gleam, the flying shower,
The rain-pools glittering on the white roads,
And shadows sweeping on from down to down
Before the salt Atlantic gale: yet come
In whatsoever garb, or gay, or sad,
Come fair, come foul, 'twill still be Christmas Day.

Christmas Morning in Exeter Cathedral

The religious celebrations in Exeter were described in this feature which appeared in the *Illustrated London News*, 25 December 1852:

The custom of welcoming this season of holy joy with 'psalms and hymns and spiritual songs' lingers in the cathedral city of Exeter where, during Christmas Eve the parish choirs perambulate the streets singing anthems, with instrumental accompaniments. The singing is protracted through the night, when the celebration often assumes a more secular character than is strictly in accordance with the festival. A more sacred commemoration is, however, at hand.

At a quarter past seven o'clock on Christmas morning the assemblage of persons in the nave of Exeter Cathedral is usually very numerous: there are the remnants of the previous vigil, with unwashed faces and sleepy eyes; but a large number are early risers, who have left their beds for better purposes than a revel. There is a great muster of the choir, and the fine Old One Hundredth Psalm is sung from the gallery to a full organ, whose billows of sound roll through the vaulted edifice. The scene is strikingly picturesque: all is dim and shadowy, the red light from the flaring candles falling upon upturned faces, and here and there falling upon a piece of graven sculpture, whilst the grey light of day begins to stream through the antique windows, adding to the solemnity of the scene. As the last verse of the Psalm peals forth, the crowd begins to move, and the spacious cathedral is soon left to the more devout few who remain to attend the morning services in the Lady Chapel.

Exeter Cathedral.

Lux Mundi - Light of the World

LUX MUNDI.

When all the stars stole to the day,
One crystal lamp still shed its ray
To hymn Chaldean Kings their way
    To Bethlehem.

As wise as rich, we may not be
In mundane love or majesty;
Yet may each soul light gloriously
    His diadem!

The Star that o'er His cradle shone,
Glad, simple straw He lay upon,
The ermin'd fields where shepherds wan
    Heard Seraphim;

The ox, the ass, their provender,
Fine gifts of gold, frankincense, myrrh,
And Mary's flow'rs that smile for her
    Are blest by Him.

Accept, we pray, our offering, Lord,
A caroll'd thanks 'fore Thee outpour'd—
That every word and every chord
    Love may impart;

And bless the meek, the poor that wait
Outside the world's imperious gate—
THY lodging they may penetrate;
    A humble heart.   D.B.

Hymn on the Nativity

A protégé of well-known author Mrs Bray, Mary Maria Colling was a servant girl from Tavistock whose charming verse on the nativity appeared in a collection of her works *Fables and other pieces in verse* (1831):

Behold he comes! The glorious King!
His blessings to diffuse;
On shining clouds the angels bring
To earth the gladd'ning news.

But there's no pomp nor state display'd
To hail him from on high;
For our salvation he has laid
His dazzling glories by.

Mary Maria Colling.

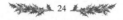

Blest Jesus! We our vows will pay:
Our grateful thanks we'll raise:
And gladly celebrate the day
With joyful songs of praise.

And when thy second advent comes,
Though bound in earth's dark bed,
At thy command, the long-closed tombs
Shall yield up all their dead.

O! may we then, with glad surprise,
Obey the dread command,
And to a life immortal rise,
And stand at thy right hand.

The Bell of Bethlehem

THE BELL OF BETHLEHEM

The bells of Christendom loud rang
  Their rounds in glad refrain;
Great Peter in the Minster sang
  Unto St. James in Spain.
From Michael's and Columba's Isles
  To Santa Fé back to St. Giles.
Cathedral towers and campaniles,
  I heard them call in madrigal
That Christ was born again.

New kings set forth with precious load
  To seek where he was born;
Poor, scatter'd riches mark the road
  That they mistook that Morn.
Till one small bell its ancient spell
  Of childhood did impart:
"Your costly burdens cast away."
  Rest here in quietude to pray
Nor gold nor gem wins Bethlehem
  But peace within the heart.

Douglas Buchanan

Christmas Bells

A poet lauded as 'the Devonshire Burns' wrote this joyous seasonal message that appeared in *Poems by Edward Capern, a rural postman of Bideford, Devon* (1856):

Ring out ye merry bells! Welcome bright icicles!
Welcome old holly-crowned Christmas again!
Blithe as a child at play, keeping his holiday,
Welcome him in from the snow-peak and plain.

Up with the holly bough, green from the winter's brow;
Lock up your ledgers and cares for a day,
Out to the forest go, gather the mistletoe,
Old and young, rich and poor, up and away.

Up with the holly bough, ay, and the laurel now,
In with the yule log, and brighten the hearth,
Quick! He is here again, come with his joyous train,
Laughter, and Music, and Friendship, and Mirth.

Up with the holly boughs, high in each manor house
Garnish the antlers that hang in the hall;
Yes, and the 'neck' of corn with a gay wreath adorn
Rich as the bloom on the cottager's wall.

Wealth has its duties now, Christians, you will allow,
Think then, ye rich, whilst your tables are spread,
Think of those wretched ones, Poverty's stricken sons,
Weeping, whilst children are asking for bread.

Edward Capern.

Ring out, ye merry bells! Ring till your music swells,
Out o'er the mountain and far on the main;
Ring till those cheerless one's catch up your merry tones,
Singing, 'Come, Christmas, again and again'.

The Christmas Bazaar

Prince Albert introduced the Christmas tree to Britain
from his native Germany and it soon became a useful
means of raising money for good causes, as shown in this
report from the *Devon Weekly Times* in December 1875:

The royal family dress the Christmas tree.

The 'Christmas tree' is an institution which rivals the bazaar as a successful means of raising money for charitable and religious purposes; and when the two are combined, the effect is correspondingly greater. The tree and bazaar are therefore very popular just now, especially with those associations – religious and otherwise – which depend on the voluntary principle for their pecuniary support; and so many are got up that one is almost inclined to wonder first where the materials for furnishing trees and stalls come from, and next how it comes that they are all so freely patronised at a time when there is such keen competition going on for loose cash. One explanation may be found in the fact that Christmas trees – rather, the mode of disposing of their burdens, and the ingenious etceteras which generally go along with them – afford some scope for a good deal of fun to those whom the Pantomime and 'such things' are tabooed. They also give the young folk opportunities for flirtation in a mild way; while to 'heads of families' they present an excuse for giving the little ones a treat, with the prospect of something 'nice' to carry home for use or admiration when Christmas-tide, with its delights and cares, its feastings and head-aches, shall once more have become a thing of the past.

The Christmas Tree

Known as 'the Hardy of Devon', prolific author Eden Phillpotts spent much of his life in Torquay, then moved to Bradninch, near Exeter, where he composed this ode published in *A Hundred Lyrics* (1930):

Eden Phillpotts.

Now opened cloudy chasms upon high
And, through the winter heaven overcast,
Shone out great stars in constellation vast,
Flashing white light on Noel Night
Steadfast across the marches of the sky.

Above the hemlock spruce, Orion hove
To twine the Hunter's girdle on its brow,
Set dewy fire in each uplifted bough
And make for me my Christmas tree,
With golden suns for little tapers rove.

O wondrous legend of humility:
That Will omnipotent, for love of man,
Shrank into flesh and suffered mortal span
And mortal scars, even as stars
Renounce their might to hang upon a tree.

The First Christmas Card

The first commercial greeting card wishing the recipient 'A
Merry Christmas and a Happy New Year' was published in
1843. The central design shows a family toasting the season,
flanked by two panels with figures depicting charitable acts
– 'feeding the hungry' and 'clothing the naked'. The artist
was John Calcott Horsley, who accepted the commission
to print a limited edition of 1,000 cards for Sir Henry Cole
– the first director of the Victoria & Albert Museum.

In 1857, Calcott took up residence at Orestone Manor, Torquay, near the estate of his brother-in-law Isambard Kingdom Brunel. While living in the town, Calcott completed a famous painting of the great engineer sitting at a desk in his library that now hangs in the National Portrait Gallery. Horsley's wife gave birth to a son on 14 April 1857 – the same day that Queen Victoria delivered the youngest of her nine children, Princess Beatrice. When the Queen heard of this happy coincidence from her head dresser, Mrs Skerrett, who was a family friend of the Horsleys, Her Majesty chose a name for the baby boy which was gratefully accepted by the delighted parents – Victor Alexander Horsley.

Old Father Christmas

This poem was written in 1850 by local author E.H. Burrington who praises the 'giver' as represented by Father Christmas. Also mentioned are the 'mummers' who entered people's houses uninvited during the festive season in the hope of receiving remuneration for miming impromptu plays re-enacting the brave deeds of St George:

> 'Father Christmas' is coming with ripe blushing holly,
> And the mistletoe clad in a magical spell;
> If the sprig in the window savours of folly,
> Still it savours of kindness and welcome as well.
> A dispenser of joy is the poor little 'mummer',

Old Father Christmas.

When he covers with tinsel the rags on his back;
In the midst of the winter he makes a new summer,
As he mimics the hero's defence or attack.

'Father Christmas' is coming, when many will shiver
As they meet the cold nights without food, without fire,
And we should not forget that God blesses the giver
Who bestows from his store what the wretched require.
If our thoughts should be lighter than many around us,
If the spirit of gladness should enter our door,
May we feel, as we thought, that old Christmas has found us
The consolers of those who are homeless and poor.

The Magic Log

A boy and girl's wish to see the magical place where Father
Christmas produces all the children's toys is answered in
this poem by Eugenie Emmett, published in the *Torquay
Times Christmas Number*, 25 December 1938:

The wind whistled shrilly
In gusts round the town,
The doors shook and rattled,
The snowflakes blew down.

And in a dark garden,
Alone in the fog,
A small boy and girl sat
Astride on a log.

'I'll hang up my stocking'
Said Teddy to Jill,
'Perhaps Father Christmas
The stocking will fill'.

'I wish I could see where
He keeps all his toys'.
Now just as he said this
They heard a queer noise.

This log shook beneath them
Moaned 'Children beware',
And, shrieking and whistling
It rose in the air.

It flew over houses
And meadows and trees,
First up, and then downwards,
Borne on by the breeze.

The children clung tightly,
Tried hard to be brave,
The log rocking wildly,
Rushed into a cave.

The cave shone and sparkled
With thousands of toys
For small girls and big girls,
For babies and boys.

And there Father Christmas,
His sledge piled up high,
Was getting it ready
To fly through the sky.
The log never stopped though,
Nor ceased its wild song,
But screaming and whistling
Flew madly along.

And out of the cave rushed,
O'er hill and o'er town,
Till back in the garden
Once more it lay down.

And Jill always tells me
This must have been true,
Or Teddy would never
Have dreamed of it too.

God Sends Meat but the Devil Sends Cooks

Isabella Beeton's famous *Book of Household Management* (1859) sold 60,000 copies in the first year of publication. By 1890, there were spin-off versions for every kind of home – from humble cottage to palatial mansion. Brides from every walk of life would ensure they had a copy of the housekeeper's bible in their kitchen. In 1899, Sir Arthur Conan Doyle wrote a study of married life entitled *A Duet, with an Occasional Chorus* in which his hero observes that Mrs Beeton's book 'has more wisdom to the square inch than any work of man' whilst his heroine concludes that 'Mrs Beeton must have been the finest housekeeper in the world. Therefore, Mr Beeton must have been the happiest and most comfortable man'.

Sadly, the latter assumption was not the case in real life, for Mrs Beeton contracted a sexually transmitted disease from her husband on their honeymoon that contributed to her premature death at the age of twenty-eight in 1865.

Sir Arthur Conan Doyle's fame was secured by the popularity of his fictional detective Sherlock Holmes who was 'killed off' by the author, then resurrected following a public outcry with the publication of his best-known work *The Hound of the Baskervilles* (1901). Set on Dartmoor, the story was inspired by legends of the Devil, known locally as Dewer, emerging from Wistman's Wood and hunting with his phantom hellhounds for the souls of unwary travellers. The unfortunate victims were pursued and driven to their deaths over the steep precipice of a rocky crag –

Sir Arthur Conan Doyle.

the Dewerstone. Dartmoor locations reflect these folktales, where 'tempting' menus of 'soul' food were prepared at the Devil's Kitchen, the Devil's Punchbowl and the Devil's Frying Pan. According to the old proverb, 'God sends meat, but the Devil sends cooks'. The basic recipes in this book are those prepared by the original 'domestic goddess', Mrs Beeton, supplemented with a series of demonic culinary 'hot tips' – with a particular penchant for advocating the liberal use of the 'evils of drink'.

The Devil's Kitchen

Situated beneath the tors of Tavy Cleve in a pool on the River Tavy where Satan keeps a lookout for tasty morsels among unwary bathers:

Roast Turkey

Prepare and truss the turkey. Fill the crop with 1-2lbs of sausage meat and put 1lb of veal forcemeat inside the body

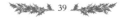

Dewer digests the wisdom of Mrs Beeton.

of the bird. Skewer two or three slices of bacon over the breast, baste well with a hot fat and roast in a moderate oven from 1½–2½ hours according to age and size of the bird. Baste frequently and, about twenty minutes before serving, remove the bacon to allow the breast to brown. Remove the trussing strings and serve on a hot dish with a sauceboat of gravy and bread sauce.

Hot Tip – Devilled Turkey With Devilled Sauce
Divide pieces of cold roast turkey into convenient sizes for serving, remove all skin and score the flesh deeply. Spread lightly with a devilled butter made with a mixture of 1oz

butter, ½ a salt spoonful each of cayenne, black pepper and curry powder, and a pinch of ground ginger. Put aside for an hour or more and allow to season as desired. Grill for approximately eight minutes and serve with a piquant devilled sauce made in a deep dish from two tablespoons of Harvey sauce, two tablespoons of vinegar, two tablespoons of melted butter, one teaspoonful each of mustard, salt and cayenne.

Christmas Pudding

To serve eight or nine persons, skin ½lb of beef suet and chop it finely. Take ½lb of raisins, ¼lb of finely shredded mixed peel, ½ a grated nutmeg, ½oz ground cinnamon, ½oz of mixed spice, ½lb breadcrumbs, ¼lb of sultanas, ¼lb of currants, the rind of a lemon, 2oz of desiccated coconut or shredded almonds, and a pinch of salt. Put all the dry ingredients into a basin and mix well. Add 1 gill of milk, stir in four eggs one at a time, add a wine glass of rum or brandy and the strained juice of the peeled lemon. Work the whole mixture thoroughly for some minutes, so that the ingredients are well blended. Put the mixture in a well-buttered basin or pudding cloth; if the latter is used, it should be buttered or floured. Boil for about four hours, or steam for at least three hours.

Hot Tip – Christmas Pudding Sauce

Place a wine glass of rum, four egg yolks, three egg whites, 2oz castor sugar and ½ gill of water into a stew pan. Stand it in a larger pan of boiling water and whisk bristly until the mixture becomes thick and frothy. Pour over the pudding and serve at once.

The Adventure of the Christmas Pudding

The custom of the traditional Christmas dinner with all the trimmings was introduced in the nineteenth century. Some illustrious Devonians from that period recorded their memories of festive feasts with a difference:

Crime novelist Agatha Christie (1890-1976) was doubtless inspired to write *The Adventure of the Christmas Pudding* by memories of glutinous feats enjoyed at her family home in Torquay. She recalled how, as a young child, she tried to out-eat the son of family friends who joined them on Christmas Day. She and her young rival, Humphrey, ate

Steaming the Christmas pudding.

solidly through the Christmas dinner. He beat her in the race to slurp down the oyster soup, but otherwise they were neck and neck. For the main course they first had roast turkey, then boiled turkey, and finally four or five slices of sirloin beef. Then followed dessert with plum pudding, mince pies and trifle – Agatha struggled with the latter as she didn't like the taste of wine. After that there were crackers, grapes, oranges, plums and preserved fruits. Finally, during the afternoon, the children gorged themselves on handfuls of chocolates and Agatha proudly survived the day without being sick or suffering from bilious attacks!

Feelings of sickness were certainly experience by mathematical genius Charles Babbage (1791-1871) after tasting an alternative feast to celebrate his birthday one Boxing Day. The boy who would later be acknowledged as the 'Father of the Computer', recalled how, when he felt he had attained manhood, he went hunting near his parent's house at Teignmouth:

> One Christmas when I was about sixteen I determined to see if I could manage a gun. I accordingly took my father's fowling-piece, and climbing with it down to the beach, I began to look about for the large sea-birds which I thought I might have a chance of hitting. I fired several charges in vain. At last, however, I was fortunate enough to hit a sea-bird called a diver; but it fell at some distance into the sea: I had no dog to get it out for me; the sea was rough, and no boat was within reach; also it was snowing. So I took advantage of a slight recess in the rock to protect my clothes from the snow, undressed, and swam out after my

Charles Babbage.

game, which I succeeded in capturing. The next day, having got the cook to roast it, I tried to eat it; but this was by no means an agreeable task, so for the future I left the sea-birds to the quiet possession of their own dominion.

Another unpleasant festive childhood experience was recalled by literary critic Edmond Gosse (1849–1928), whose family's religious convictions caused him to suffer pangs of guilt for devouring a forbidden portion of plum pudding. His father, marine biologist Phillip Gosse, was a member of the Plymouth Brethren and banned seasonal festivities in their Torquay home:

On Christmas Day of this year 1857 our villa saw a very unusual sight. My father had given strictest charge that no difference whatever was to be made in our meals on that day; the dinner was to be neither more copious than usual nor less so. He was obeyed, but the servants, secretly rebellious, made a small plum pudding for themselves. … Early in the afternoon, the maids - of whom we were now advanced to keeping two - kindly remarked that 'the poor dear child ought to have a bit, anyhow', and wheedled me into the kitchen, where I ate a slice of plum pudding. Shortly I began to feel that pain inside which in my frail state was inevitable, and my conscience smote me violently. At length I could bear my spiritual anguish no longer, and bursting into the study I called out: 'Oh! Papa, Papa, I have eaten of flesh offered to idols!' It took me some time, between my sobs, to explain what had happened. Then my father sternly said: 'Where is the accursed thing?' I explained that as much as was left of it was still on the kitchen table. He took me by the hand, and ran with me into the midst of the startled servants, seized what remained of the pudding, and with the plate in one hand and me still tight in the other, ran till we reached the dust-heap, when he flung the idolatrous confectionary on to the middle of the ashes, and then raked it deep down into the mass. The suddenness, the violence, the velocity of this extraordinary act made an impression on my memory which nothing will ever efface.

If ever a true life adventure involving a Christmas pudding occurred, it was in 1902 when Plymouth's Captain Robert Falcon Scott (1868-1912) took part in an unsuccessful attempt to reach the South Pole with Sir Ernest Shackleton, who conjured up a Christmas Day surprise to raise the morale of his fellow polar explorer:

I had observed Shackleton ferreting about in his bundle, out of which he presently produced a spare sock. Stored away in that sock was a small round object about the size of a cricket ball, which when brought to light, proved to be a notable plum pudding. Another dive into his lucky bag and out came a crumpled piece of artificial holly. Heated in the cocoa, our plum pudding was soon steaming hot, and stood on the cooker-lid crowned with its decoration. Our Christmas Day had proved a delightful break in an otherwise uninterrupted spell of semi-starvation. Some days elapsed before its pleasing effects wore off.

The Prize Turkey

In December 1892, a correspondent of the *Western Daily Mercury* paid this cynical tribute to a farming 'genius' who had cheated him over the weight of a turkey:

A Plymouth householder's Christmas experience prompts him to ask whether the farmers of Devon and Cornwall have heard of the latest remedy for agricultural depression. We are told, he says, that corn can no longer be grown at a profit, that beef and mutton are poor reeds to lean upon, and that the British farmer must look to poultry raising and a few other things of that sort for salvation. Poultry is bound to pay, our correspondent thinks, if managed on the same principle as the turkey that graced his board on Christmas Day. He was a fine bird but rather heavy for his size. An investigation of his interior explained the reason:

'Well, Garge, did you sell the prize turkey?'
'Ay… But I didn't get as much as I expected – but I
didn't expect to'.

for it brought to light the fact that the bird's natural weight
had been increased by the addition to its contents of over a
pound weight of small shot! The man who fed that turkey,
says our correspondent, ought to read a paper on the raising of poultry before the Devon and Cornwall Chamber
of Agriculture. He is a genius. Shots cost more than corn
weight, no doubt, but then it lasts longer and when sold as
dead turkey at a shilling a pound, it brings a clear profit of
at least 100 per cent!

Heaven in Devon

Known as 'My Lady of the Moor', former nun Beatrice Chase devoutly believed that the River Dart periodically gave a 'cry' at Broad Stone which signalled the imminent death of an un-baptised child. In a lighter vein, the writer used the same setting for a woman in love's cry which united two hearts in this romantic short story which appeared in the *Torquay Times Christmas Issue*, 25 December 1927:

Susan Southwood sat on the lower end of Broad Stone gazing at the torrents of water roaring through the narrow channel where the Dart makes her world-famed cry for a heart.

The river was in flood and had been so churned, torn, and obstructed by rocks on its course from Cranmere Pool, that the mighty cataracts thundering past Broad Stone were like huge snowdrifts, for hardly anything could be seen in the mad whirl but piled up masses of beaten foam.

On the left, Bench Tor reared his seal brown hulk, which was crowned at the summit by a light powdering of snow against the violet blue of the sky. Not a dead leaf stirred. The sun poured down into the deep high ravine with a strength and clearness never attained in mist-shot, storm-haunted summer.

The whole colouring was rich russet, deep brown, grey, white and blue, besides the gold flashing from myriad points of the river, the little melted pools on the rocks, and the wet foliage of trees in Mel Tor woods.

Beatrice Chase – My Lady of
the Moor.

It was rarely that Susan found time to descend to Broad
Stone, but her Christmas arrangements were so well on,
and the day had been so exceptionally lovely, that she had
yielded to temptation, especially as she did not know when
she might be free to return.

The lodger would arrive tomorrow. Being a normal
young woman, Susan's thoughts were full of the unknown
man who, by next evening, would be living under her roof.
Susan and her pretty younger sister Alice now lived alone
at Southbrook Cottage, and had been forced that year,
through increased cost of living and some necessary repairs
to the cottage roof, to take in lodgers. So they were still
new to the game and still wholeheartedly interested in everyone who came.

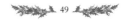

But this was the first time they had ventured on a lonely man. He had answered their advertisement in one of the county papers, and had explained that he was just home from Canada and longing to see the old place again.

Susan and Alice felt a special interest in him because of his letter. They did not know whether he was young or old, married or single, rich or poor. All they knew was that he was a fellow Devonian returning from a long exile for Christmas in the old country.

'And I reckon he haven't seen anywhere as lovely as this in all the miles he's travelled', said Susan to the Dart, as she reluctantly rose to return.

At sunset next evening, the stranger arrived. He was a sunburnt, healthy-looking man of nearly forty, and he said, or rather his first letter had said, his name was Roderick Grant.

He cast a searching glance around as he alighted from the station car, and with the glance, took in the homely old-world beauty of the little low thatched cottage, with its whitened walls, green windows, through one of which scarlet light was flashing from the fire on the wide open hearth inside.

'What a picture!' he laughed, advancing bareheaded to meet Susan. It was she who always greeted newcomers. Alice saved her charms till the visitors had seen everything else and got acclimatised, so to speak, from other distractions.

'How do you do, Miss Southwood? I do hope you have got cream and jam and currant loaf for tea – the real Dartmoor tea that I used to have as a boy'.

Christmas chuckles -
'Mamma, is it called
Kissmas Time because
everybody kisses under
the mistletoe?'

He looked laughingly into the bright brown eyes set in
the smooth face which was the colour and texture of a
damask rose.

'Yes sir, that's just what us have got. 'Tis the usual thing'.

'Thank heaven for that', exclaimed the stranger piously.
'I was afraid every old custom would be swept away'.

Susan duly left him alone with the steaming and fra-
grant brown teapot, and with injunctions to ring the little
hand-bell when he had finished. Then she retired to the
old-fashioned cottage kitchen, where Alice was ironing,
with becoming blush on her pretty face, which made the
blue eyes still more blue.

'You can clean up when he rings. He's a proper man',
began Susan. 'No-one haven't cared so much at first sight.
'Tis nice getting lets in wintertime', she continued thank-
fully. 'Time living be dearest and coal so much wanted and

all. But, after that, if folk only knew it, winter's the loveliest time on Dartmoor. 'Twas grand at Broad Stone today'.

'Was Dart crying?' asked Alice, idly, as she picked up another handkerchief.

'No'.

In due time came the tinkle of the bell, and with a toss of her golden ringlets, Alice went into the little parlour to be greeted by the same pleasant praise of the tea, the cake, the cream, the log fire, and the view from the window. For a man of his age, the stranger appeared as enthusiastic as any boy.

Several days went by. The fine weather held and Mr Grant was out, early and late, getting more sunburnt, reddened by the keen wind and revelling in the moor.

On the fourth morning, the sisters heard a yell of horror from his room, followed by a quickly opened door.

'Miss Southwood. I'm so sorry. Like the clumsy fool I am, I've upset my shaving mug, and the drawer was open, and it's splashed all over everything'.

Seizing a duster, Susan ran up, uttering coos and murmurs of sympathy.

She removed ties, collars and socks, and ran down to put them on the clothes-horse before the kitchen fire to dry. Then, when Mr Grant was safely occupied with his breakfast of bacon and succulent brown fried 'tetties', she returned to make up his bed and reline the drawer with dry newspaper.

Susan rolled up the wet paper, rubbed the drawer with a clean duster, and then unfolded the clean sheets and proceeded to line them into the exact size of the drawer bottom. As she did so, she caught sight of her own advertisement and smiled.

'Wonder if many be advertising and if they've got such a nice visitor as what we have', she thought, pausing to glance down the sparse column of 'Furnished Apartments Vacant'. No other Dartmoor advertisement, any way. The rest were mostly in the neighbourhood of Torquay. Idly her glance travelled down the 'Miscellaneous' column, and she gave a gasp of astonishment. In quite large print stood the announcement, 'If any relative of James Roderick Grant will communicate with Messrs, Sele and Deedes, Plymouth, they may hear of something to their advantage'.

Susan's heart set off thumping at an unparalleled rate. She turned over the paper to glance the date. It was an old one of the previous May.

Horrified, she let it drop, then picked it up and re-read the announcement. Of course, if it was anything to do with her Mr Grant, he would have seen and answered long ago, and probably that explained his presence in England and upon Dartmoor.

She finished the room, then picked up the paper and found Alice.

The girl became greatly excited. 'Of course you must show it to him. We don't know that he's seen it. May be just providence like'.

Susan shook her head. She was not, like Alice, abreast of contemporary fiction, and she was unaware that real life is stranger, more improbable, than any written plot.

Mr Grant was leisurely filling his pipe with his back to the room, and his eyes straying to the grand hog back of

Bench Tor – Benjy, as he is familiarly called by the denizens of Dartmoor.

'I haven't been yet to Broad Stone, Miss Southwood', he said, turning with his usual bright smile. 'I am saving that for a day when you yourself can take me'.

Susan blushed. She could not remember ever going alone for a walk with a strange gentleman, and the prospect stirred unknown depths within her placid heart.

'Please sir, I've found this in an old newspaper. But I reckon you know all about it', she said handing him the folded sheet.

He glanced down, started, and a look of blank amazement swept over his face.

'No, indeed. Good gracious. James Roderick Grant was my great uncle, who owned that desolate old farm out beyond Fox Tor mires, donkey's years ago. Whatever can he have had to leave anyone?'

''Tis an old paper', repeated Susan in a faltering voice. 'Reckon everything's fixed up by now. Fancy, you not having seen it, sir'.

Mr Grant dropped the paper and fixed a piercing but entirely abstracted gaze upon his handsome hostess.

'I don't know', he said, in the monotonous tone of a seer. 'There aren't such a mighty lot of Grants or ever were for that matter. My father was an only child and he had only one great uncle – this old Uncle Jim. My grandfather died when my father was a baby, and my father had only two children, myself and my sister Ethel, who is married out in Canada. So, you see, unless some very distant branch turns up, there aren't exactly what you would call a crowd of us'.

'No, sir', faltered Susan, 'Beg pardon, sir, if I am making too free but are you married too?'

The stranger fixed her with a searching, and this time conscious glance. 'No', he answered slowly. 'Not yet, but I hope to be soon'.

Susan was shocked at a cold pang of which crept through her. Of course, it was due to hearing that there was no chance of a good husband for Alice. Of course, that would be the reason. Of course. Mr Grant was considering the calendar.

'December the 23rd', he remarked. 'Lawyers' offices don't shut till tonight and some are open, I believe, in the morning of the 24th. Anyway, we'll try a telegram'. And he was off.

Susan returned to her sister who seemed much moved by the news of their visitor's impending marriage.

'Lucky maid her'll be', she sighed; 'specially if these lawyer gentlemen have got anything worth giving to him'.

Mr Grant did not return till evening and bore with Spartan fortitude the news that there had been no reply to his telegram.

Next day was as lovely as ever, and he went out with his lunch for a long tramp.

At noon the sisters were startled by the sound of a car and grinding brakes outside their green wicket gate.

'Oh, my dear life', exclaimed Susan. 'I hope it baint new lodgers for one night, or something, just at Christmas, with market over and all shops shut'.

Her lamentations were cut short by the sight of a bobbed auburn head, surmounted by a jaunty hat of black fur.

 55

An attractive girl was dismounting from the car and making for the door of the cottage.

'Good morning', she smiled sighting Susan. 'Is Mr Grant here?'

Another cold pang shot through Susan. This, this, of course, was his sweetheart come to spend Christmas with him.

'Yes, miss, but he be out at present and won't be back till teatime'.

'Bother!' exclaimed the girl, swinging round and gazing at the car for inspiration. 'I didn't know anyone was ever out for so long on Dartmoor, especially in winter. And I promised daddy to be over by three o'clock'.

She paused, and then turned to the palpitating Susan, eyeing her with disconcerting severity. 'May I ask who you are?'

'I am – my name is Southwood – Susan Southwood. I let rooms, and Mr Grant is staying here for a time. He answered our advertisement'.

'I see. Well, if you could give him a message. You perhaps know that we, my father, that is, has been advertising for his family. My name is Sele'.

'Yes, oh yes', faltered Susan. She was trying to work out how Mr Grant was going to marry Miss Sele if he had never heard of the firm before, and the effort was too much for her agitated intelligence.

'If you could tell him', she found her pretty visitor saying, with a touch of severity in her voice, 'that my father asked me to call as I was crossing the moor today to say we have had, or he has had Mr Grant's telegram, and if

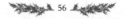

Mr Grant can prove his identity and there is no nearer of kin, the old Mr Grant had some waste land near Fox Tor which has developed into valuable peat works, and there is also the little house and farm buildings, and so on'.

She paused. Really, this handsome daughter of Dartmoor seemed half-witted or something.

'Yes miss, yes', answered Susan hurriedly. 'I'll tell him. Anything else, miss?'

'Yes, please explain that I act as shorthand typist clerk to my father, which is why I am mixed up with it, and my father would like Mr Grant to call on us on the 28th. The office won't be open before then'.

She turned and got into her car and two minutes later was whizzed away, leaving Susan gasping.

Susan was still muddled when Mr Grant came home, but she managed to convey an accurate message which her visitor greeted with a long whistle of amazement.

'Peat works! Well, well. One doesn't become a bloated millionaire on peat, but still, it's an annual income and an old Dartmoor farm, a homestead in the old enchanted land, which is worth more than its weight in gold to me'.

He fell into a happy reverie and Susan withdrew, a prey to conflicting and indescribable emotions.

Christmas Day was a quietly happy one, with the brilliant sunshine, white frost, and the sound of church bells rising and falling on the light breeze.

The Christmas dinner at midday was a huge success, and Mr Grant had previously insisted on their having it together.

He carved the turkey and Susan cut the hard black plum pudding with a spasm of relief that it hadn't broken

in turning out, and though hard, was as light as Christmas pudding should be.

During the meal, Mr Grant paid Alice some pretty compliments, and talked laughingly of his coming luck, toasting it and his new home with the real 'Demsur' draught cider.

After dinner he turned to Susan.

'Miss Southwood. I have set my heart on going to Broad Stone today. You can't disappoint me. I'll wash up all day tomorrow for you rather than miss the walk this afternoon. You will come?'

Susan glanced doubtfully at Alice, who looked anything but pleasant.

'You go to Mrs Warren's, dear, to hear the carols on the wireless, same as they asked you, and leave everything, leave the lot, and I'll do it when I get back'.

'Thank you, I will'. said Alice, tossing her head. 'I might as well enjoy myself too, and Tom will be there'.

So in a comparatively short space of time, the man and the maid stood upon the old-world Broad Stone. For a long time Mr Grant did not speak. Then, at last, he turned with a smile, and taking Susan's unresisting hand, led her back along the bank to a sheltered boulder under the cliff side.

'God has been good to me', he said very simply, 'It was inspiration my deciding to come to see old England for a holiday, and providence which led me to see your adver-tisement and you to see Mr Deedes's. The links forged by the Divine Hand in human lives are indeed beautiful and wonderful, and one feels them so much at this time of the year – the anniversary of His coming down to mix Himself in the affairs of humanity'.

'Yes', murmured Susan, conscious of a rush of joy at the man's childlike faith.

'Do you believe in the old saying:' Marriages are made in heaven?', he asked next.

Susan glanced at him, blushing mightily, and lowered her eyes. 'Of course'.

'Well, Providence has shown such an interest in my story that it won't let me down over the crowning point. I told you I hoped soon to be married. I do. I hope soon to marry you'.

Susan gave an inarticulate cry which was drowned, stifled against a broad shoulder belonging to an arm that went reverently round her waist.

'Susan you are the kind of woman that any man with eyes in his head loves at sight. You are the kind of woman he wants to be his own and the mother of his children. And, in addition to that, you are specially linked with me seeing it was you who found my luck for me. Yes, marriages are made in heaven all right. But as Devon is next door to heaven, the marriages, some of them, materialise in Devon'.

Christmas Decorations

The Vicar of Dean Prior, Robert Herrick, warns in *Hesperides* (1648) that leaving decorations up beyond the Twelve Days of Christmas will result in the home being invaded by a plague of mischievous ugly elves:

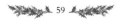 59

The Christmas holly cart.

Down with the rosemary, and so,
Down with the bais and mistletoe:
Down with the holly, ivie, all,
Wherewith you drest the Christmas hall:
That so the superstitious find
No one least branch there left behind.
For look how many leaves there be
Neglected there (maids, trust to me),
So many goblins you shall see.

The Holy Ghost of Lapford

This is the story of a Devonian nobleman's involvement in
the assassination of Thomas Beckett:

On Christmas Day 1170, the long-standing feud
between Henry II and the Archbishop of Canterbury,
Thomas Becket, finally erupted when news reached the
King at his court in France that Becket, recently reinstated
after spending six years in exile, had excommunicated the
bishops who had officiated at Henry's coronation during
his absence. According to these bishops, Becket was ready
to 'tear the crown from the young king's head'. The monarch was enraged, 'What a pack of fools and cowards have I
nourished in my household' he cried, 'that not one of them
will avenge me of this turbulent priest'.

William de Tracy, Reginald fitzUrse, Hugh de Murville,
and Richard le Breton were stung into action by this out-
burst and immediately set sail for England, believing they
had the King's blessing. The four knights rode to Canterbury.
When they entered the Archbishop's chamber, Sir William
de Tracy was the only one whom Thomas recognised and
greeted by name. A ferocious argument ensued and the
knights left to arm themselves. They returned to the cathedral an hour later to carry out their vow to slay Becket. Tracy
strode forward and warned, 'Flee! Thou art death's man', but
was seized by the Archbishop who flung him aside. Several
sword blows then rained down on the defenceless churchman and Tracy struck the fatal blow, slicing off the crown of
his head and causing his brains to spill out onto the floor.

The assassination of Thomas Beckett.

Becket's death sealed the self-fulfilling prophesy he had made when first offered the post by his former friend Henry, 'Should God permit me to be Archbishop I should lose Your Majesty's favour'. Their quarrels had stemmed from the issue of whether the State or Church should have jurisdiction in ecclesiastical matters, particularly in the case of a lawbreaking cleric's right to be tried in church courts. The Archbishop's murder provoked great indignation across Europe and miracles reportedly occurred to pilgrims visiting Becket's tomb. In 1173, the pope canonised Thomas and King Henry was forced to visit Canterbury to pay penance, where he was ceremonially whipped by monks as he left the abbey. Immediately after the murder, William de Tracy returned to his own diocese and made a confession to Bishop Bartholomew of Exeter, then surrendered himself to the Pope's mercy. He and his fellow conspirators were ordered to spend fourteen years with the Templars and adhere to a lifelong penance of fasting and prayer. Tracy set out for the Holy Land in 1173, but according to an unsubstantiated medieval account, got no further than Cosenza in Sicily. There he is said to have contracted a terrible wasting disease and died in agony, tearing away the decaying flesh from his body whilst praying incessantly for forgiveness from St Thomas. On his deathbed he made out a charter granting his Devon manor of Doccombe to the Chapter of Canterbury 'for the love of God, the salvation of my own soul and my ancestors' souls, and for the love of the blessed Thomas, Archbishop and martyr, of venerable memory'.

The de Tracy family hailed from the Norman village of Traci near Bayeaux. The family seat in Devon was located at Morthoe and it seems probable that Henry de Tracy was granted the Barony of Barnstaple during the reign of Henry II's predecessor, King Stephen. William de Tracy's pedigree is uncertain, but there is a compelling theory that his grandfather was sired by Henry I, who publicly acknowledged only twenty of his numerous illegitimate offspring. Therefore, this branch of the de Tracy family took the mother's name and held the Baronies of Woollacombe and Bradninch. Following the death of Thomas Becket, all members of the de Tracy family felt shamed and undertook charitable work in the county to atone for the wrongdoing.

Despite the fact that there is no evidence that Thomas Becket ever visited Devon, there is an intriguing myth associated with William de Tracy's motives for taking part in the assassination. The tale relates how the Archbishop visited

Buckfast Abbey and later journeyed to Bovey Tracey where he was entertained by de Tracy and his wife. Later, while her husband was attending King Henry's court in France, Lady de Tracy invited the churchman to counsel her on religious matters, but this was misconstrued by Sir William who believed these liaisons were evidence of an affair. After the grim deed, Sir William retreated to Morthoe and sent for his wife, who was horrified to learn of her husband's misguided jealousy. The shock of Becket's death caused her to go into premature labour and the couple's son was stillborn. Filled with remorse for doubting the integrity of Lady de Tracy and Sir Thomas, William decided to erect churches dedicated to the memory of the saint at Morthoe, Bovey Tracy and Barnstaple.

According to legend, William de Tracy broke his sword as a gesture of remorse and threw it into the river. The pieces were found and welded together and put on display at the Riverside Hotel in Bovey Tracey. Devonians have another constant reminder of William de Tracy's treachery, for the ghost of St Thomas Becket gallops through the village of Lapford on his way to Nymet Tracey at midnight on each anniversary of his death.

two

YULETIDE TIPPLES
AND SPIRITS

A Devonshire Ghost Story

Christmas time is associated with celebratory drinking and relating ghost stories. The two pastimes are often linked, as in this variation on the common theme of a drunk in a graveyard who is mistaken for a ghost. It was written by G. Seague and published in the *Devon Weekly Times*, Christmas Eve 1896:

It was a Christmas of the old fashioned sort. The snow lay thick, crisp, and white upon the ground while the red berries gleamed out in bright profusion from their fantastic setting of rich green leaves – leaves which contrasted strongly with the dainty delicately tinted mistletoe which hung over the doorway of the quaint, but not very commodious, school room which constituted the most important building in a small Devonshire town. It was a picturesque portion of the county, which has now been touched by the railway line, but which, at the time of my story, stood, as it were, within a little world of its own, jealously cherishing its time honoured traditions and clinging to its old world customs. The little world thus indicated was agitated by a flutter of exhilaration more than usually pronounced even at that joyous season by the fact that to the Christmas festivities were added those attendant upon the coming of age of good old Squire Western's eldest son, the heir to Thornley.

There had been a mighty consumption of roast beef and plum pudding and a prodigious quantity of 'Old October' brewed specially for the auspicious event, and which had a reputation of having attained an age equivalent to that at

Devon's most famous folk song, 'Widecombe Fair'.

which the prospective squire had arrived, and disappeared. Toast and singing had flown merrily round, and a jolly looking young fellow, with a fresh healthy complexion and a frank open countenance was relating, more or less musically, the adventures of certain persons who borrowed an old grey mare from an obliging friend whom they familiarly styled 'Tom Pearse' and who, consistent with tradition, lost both his beast and his friends as the result of his trustfulness.

The poet thus describes the sad sequel to the generosity of friend Tom:

When the wind whistles cold on the moor of a night.
All along, down along, out along lee.
Tom Pearse's old mare doth appear ghastly white,
Wi' Bill Brewer, Jan Stewer, Peter Gurney,
Peter Davy, Dan Whiddon,
Harry Hawke and Old Uncle Tom Cobley and all,

And all the long night be heard skirling and groans.
From Tom Pearse's old mare in her rattling bones,
And from Bill Brewer &c

The Singing of the old Devonshire ditty, which enabled
its bearers to indulge in long chorus, repeated after each
two or three lines of narrative verse, was followed by hearty
applause and some laughter, upon which a venerable old
villager – the real, live, oldest inhabitant of the neighbourhood – chimed in about certain rustic and highly
respectable ghosts who had come within the scope of his
experience, including that of a deceased tom cat who had
been a venerable retainer in his father's house, and whose
spirit form was always to be seen and its voices heard in
woeful caterwauling when death was about to visit the
household.

A stalwart young policeman was standing near the door,
ostensibly for the purpose of seeing that everything was
carried out 'with decency and in order' but who evidently
seemed more anxious to take into custody the smart little
waitress from the 'Cat and Fiddle' who was whisking
about with the good things in requisition. But he had a
rival in young Bob Stemson, the lad who had just been
singing, and both were intent upon winning the smile of
the comely daughter of the local carrier – Long Luke, as
he was called, from the extreme longitude of his propor-
tions. Mr Luke was not what might be generally regarded
as an ideal father-in-law. He drank huge quantities of ale,
smoked like a volcano in eruptions and was of an erratic
an disagreeable temper. Still, the charms of the daughter

more than outweighed, in the opinion of her admirers, the defects of the father. On the occasion in question Long Luke had partaken plenteously of the good cheer provided and after waxing argumentative for a time had subsided into a state of peaceful somnolence, from which he was not aroused until nearly all the company had dispersed.

At twelve o'clock that night Constable Davey was perambulating his lonely beat. A portion of the ground which he had to cover led through the churchyard, and as he drew near to this portion of his peregrinations thoughts arose within him of the ghost stories which the old folks had related at that day's merrymaking. His previous meditations had been of the trim little lass from whom he had snatched a kiss, under the mistletoe, when 'no one was looking' unconscious of the fact that young Stemson had preceded him by only a few moments in a similar clandestine operation. To turn from dreams so bright to ghostly considerations was not pleasant, but feelings will sometimes come over one in a churchyard, at the dead of night, which would not trouble one in the brightness and beauty of day.

The 'midnight bell' had 'with its iron tongue and brazen mouth' sounded twelve 'unto the dreary race of night' and the last note was just dying away when the ear of the constable was arrested by a sound which seemed to proceed from below the surface of the ground not far from where he stood. It was as though some unquiet spirit was seeking to break through the confines of the grave. Petrified with superstitious dread, the constable gazed in the direction of the sound.

The soft rays of the moon were filtered on to a grassy mound through weird-looking trees which dropped over

Christmas chuckles – A direct hit!

it, and by its light the constable saw at first a long, bony, claw-like hand protruding from the ground, then another, and then – oh, horrors of horrors – a livid, death-like head, in which were set deep, sinister, piercing eyes, which seemed to glare fiercely at the terrified onlooker. At first, the constable stood as one rooted to the spot, paralysed with fear and deprived of the power of motion. Then, with a fearful yell, he rushed madly from the spot.

Morning had dawned, and the pleasant haunts of the elves and pixies of Devonshire's fairyland – those mischievous imps which are said to have led so many good and true yeomen astray when returning from market to their hearths, their homes and their good dames – were basking in the kindly glances of honest old Sol, who was doing his best to wage successful battle with that terribly mischievous fellow, Jack Frost. A choice company were quaffing their ale and smoking 'churchwardens' in the snug little parlour of the 'Cat and Fiddle'.

The topic of conversation was the adventure of Constable Davey, who, it was said, had seen a ghost in the churchyard, and who was now laid up on account of the shock to his nervous system. The story was being narrated for the fortieth time, when a newcomer arrived in the form of Long Luke.

'Well', said he, 'I've heard tell uv sum curyis things in me time, but thicky thare yarn o' yourn bayts cock-vighting'.

'Cock-vighting or hoss-racing: tis true, that's sartin. There's the bobby haum to es lodgins, purty near vrightened to death'.

'Ah', said Luke, with more than usual satisfaction in his tone, 'I'll zune lay tha ghost and cure the bobby tu. Whey, thic ghost was me'.

'You?' chorused the astonished audience.

'Ees, sure'. And then he told a story – which was, in effect, that coming through the churchyard on his way home from the festivities of the previous day he fell into an open grave, and remained unconscious for some time. Awaking, and finding his quarters far from comfortable, he hastened to get out. This he was in a fair way of doing, by inserting his toes into the mound on either side and thus raising himself to the surface, when just as he got his head above ground he was nearly frightened out of his wits by hearing an unearthly yell and seeing a huge black figure bounding across the ground.

'And that', added he, in conclusion, 'wuz tha' p'leeceman. Wull, I'm danged! I shull marry my darter to Bob Stemson. Et zhant be zed that old Luke givved away his gal to a veller that runned auf an left es pore old vather-en-law in tha' grave'.

And he kept his word.

The Wassailing

By Eden Phillpotts from *A Dish of Apples* (1921). An abridged version of a poem about the ancient tradition of 'wassailing' which ensures a bumper crop of apples at the next harvest. Locals visit an orchard either on Christmas Eve or Twelfth Night where they drink mulled cider and fire shotguns through the branches to wake the trees up from their winter sleep:

Old Christmas Eve's the proper night
For Wassailing the apple trees;
And though the snow came to their knees,
Our fore-fathers done what was right,
Poured out their cider, sang their song
And fired their guns the boughs among.

The girls their cider pitchers bring,
With liquor steaming on the air

Wassailing in Devon.

And toast and spices floating there.
Then come a score of boys to sing,
And at the gate awaiting us,
Jan Bassett with his blunderbuss.

Bang! Bang! And Bang! The guns do ring
And flash a light upon the throng,
Who laugh aloud and tramp along
All busy at the wassailing.
But here and there twin shadows go
Where hangs a tod of mistletoe.

The moony branches, bright and clear
Are full of funny, goblin eyes
All staring down in great surprise
To see their neighbours keep such cheer.

There's whispering from tree to tree
Above the jolly company.

Yet when Old Christmas Eve do bring
Together moon and snow once more,
I see that far away upstore;
I hear the sleeping people sing,
And mark, so thick as honey bees,
Their ghosts through the apple-trees.

Devonshire Cider

Award-winning *Tarka the Otter* author Henry Williamson witnessed the age-old festive custom of 'wassailing' after moving to Devon. He relished the opportunity to try and impress the locals by producing his own cask of 'Demsur' Cider:

Born in London, Henry Williamson (1895-1977) developed a love of nature during his childhood. A remarkable writing career was put on hold as he served with the London Rifle Brigade during the First World War. Profoundly affected by the futility of the conflict, a glimmer of hope for mankind occurred during the famous 'Christmas Truce' of 1914. Williamson was stationed in the bloody trenches of Flanders, where troops spontaneously sang carols on Christmas Eve. Next morning, Williamson witnessed how a Christmas tree appeared on the parapet behind the German lines, before a soldier emerged and called out,

CIDER MAKING

WHEN God decreed the apple
  His purposes were clear:
To make the orchards pink-and-white
  When Spring at last is here;
And, when the summer months have
    rolled,
To bend the boughs with burnished gold
For doctors, passing, to behold
  And think of fees with fear.

When God decreed the apple
  That press He also planned
Which squeezes out the amber juice
  Beneficent and bland:
The juice that cheers when life seems vain,
The juice that makes you laugh again,
So come and drain a mug or twain
  Down in the cider land!

'Come over Tommy, come over Tommy'. Hostilities were gleefully postponed as men from both sides began mingling, laughing, talking and exchanging souvenirs. Laying down their arms for Christmas, troops even arranged a football match and engaged happily in a sporting 'battle'. Despite the fervent belief of all combatants that they were fighting for 'King and Country' this extraordinary occurrence, in tribute to the birth of the 'Prince of Peace', proved to be a 'revelation' to Williamson. He wrote, 'I have never forgotten that Christmas Day. I suppose it was one of the greatest moments of my life… Of course many battles intervened. But the spirit of that time remained with me and my comrades'.

This experience determined his life's work – to oppose war by showing the world, through his writing, that truth and peace lay in the gift of nature. In 1921, Williamson settled in the village of Georgeham where he had spent childhood holidays with his aunt. Exmoor and the surrounding North Devon countryside was to inspire several works, including his masterpiece, *Tarka the Otter* (1927). Anyone born outside the county in those days was looked upon as a 'foreigner' and it took some time for the writer to become accepted as a 'proper' villager. Having done so, he proudly assumed the mantle of the 'serious historian of the village' and published his reminiscences in *The Village Book* (1930). One of the most amusing recollections occurred when he decided to prove his worth to his rustic neighbours by embracing the age-old custom of cider-making. The results were to prove hilariously disastrous.

Having been given several sacks of apples one autumn, Williamson took a nine-gallon sherry cask and a motley mixture of apples piled up in a wheelbarrow. He then approached Farmer Rudd in Ham, who owned a 'modern' cider press erected by his grandfather, a massive 'oaken engine' with twin-screwed rods of iron at each end of the press. The thick rods allowed the press to run up and down with level ease on their greased threads. The farmer was glad to oblige the novice brewer and, with the help of his brother, tipped the apples into the cutting machine. While the brother turned the handle, the farmer pressed the apples down with a spade, but the 'bob-bob-bobble' of the hard apples against the blunt revolving knives presented a problem. The two experts struggled for several minutes and the supplier began to feel embarrassed as sweat appeared on their brows in an effort to break the apples and release the precious juice. Williamson apologised for the quality of his apples, but the farmer replied, 'Don't 'ee worry, they'm hard, that's why they be 'opping but us'll get'n through in a while, when the acid eats into the knives'. This theory proved a forlorn hope and eventually the operatives were forced to smash the apples with a wooden mallet. The manufacturing process could now begin in earnest, for once broken from their smoothness, the crushed apples were drawn into the rusty knives and chewed into fragments. Shovelfuls of fruit were then placed under the press, and built up into what is called the cheese. First a layer of apple fragments, then a layer of straw, with the ends turned up and tucked over the layer, then more apple fragments, then more straw. The cheese was squeezed down, then the oak press was spun upwards and more layers of straw and apples built up. So it went on, until all that remained of three sacks of apples was a flat and hard wad of pulped straw, pips, cores and skin, which was lifted off and thrown to chickens belonging to a neighbour called Billy Goldsworthy.

The clouded apple juice in the kieve, or trough, below was then poured into an oaken butt to be left to settle. Later it would be racked, or siphoned into a barrel lying on its side with the bung-hole open at the top. As the author did not have sufficient apple juice to fill the barrel, the farmer added some of his own stock until it was filled, explaining that it was necessary for the barrel to be bung-full for the scum of the first fermentation to froth up and dribble away. After a week, when this first fermentation ceased, the cider was ready for racking off into the sherry cask. At this point Williamson was away from home. Therefore, Farmer Rudd tapped the bung well home and Billy Goldsworthy kindly took the cask to the Williamson family cottage and placed it in the cellar.

Six months later, when the writer tapped the cask on a hot March day, he watched in anticipation as 'a thick brownish-bubbling stream like varnish ran forth, silently, amidst a swarm of un-burst bubbles'. Seeing Billy Goldsworthy passing by, the excited cider-maker invited him in to taste the results of his labours, insisting that he be the first to taste it, having generously transported the cider free of charge in his wheel-barrow.

Billy Goldsworthy took hold of the jug and sniffed it suspiciously. Then he grimaced as he took a sip of the obnoxious smelling liquid which, in his considered

Christmas chuckles – 'Sorry sir, I was aiming at my friend!'

opinion, tasted like 'a swarm of bees about the tongue'. Williamson had to agree that the cider was ruined and there was nothing for it but to roll the barrel outside the gate and empty its gurgling contents down the dusty road which ran through the village. However, the intoxicating effects of the aroma rising from the rivulets soon became apparent when Williamson felt increasingly light-headed. He lost his inhibitions and began flirting outrageously with his wife in front of the housemaid. Several neighbours complained of headaches and others became uncharacteristically argumentative with each other. Williamson also noticed the strange effect that the cider had on the insect life that paused to sample the alcoholic nectar. In a stupor, several bluebottles and large queen wasps were crawling over the damp cider marks in the road. When he touched one with a stick, it was too drunk to fly.

Explanations were readily offered about what may have gone wrong with the cider. Billy Goldsworthy suggested that it needed 'iron' and might have been passable if the brewer had employed the well-known trick of adding an old iron chain or a bag of old nails. The village butcher contended that the brew required 'meat' and would have benefited from placing several dead rats in the barrel. To which the author mischievously retorted that he was making cider not 'sausages'.

Disappointed at his humiliating failure, Henry Williamson, determined 'to dislike cider forever'. Having produced his first and last cask, he denounced farmhouse cider as a 'filthy poison' and recalled one of the many popular ballads praising the dubious pleasures of 'Devonshire Cider':

> Hard cider much as you please
> Loose your teeth and bow your knees
> Sour your gut and make you wheeze
> Turn your words to sting of bees
> Thin your blood and kill your fleas
> Hard cider much as you please

The Merry Carol Singers

In 1881, the Reverend Sabine Baring-Gould, squire and rector of Lew Trenchard, recalled an earlier Christmas in the ancestral home that appeared in *Further Reminiscences 1864-1894* (1925):

Alone, except for my little brother, in Lew House. The rats are celebrating Noel. They had a frolic last night, kept high festival, had a wild hunt. They scoured along the passages, they scampered between floor and ceiling, they danced a hornpipe in the storeroom and rollicked up and down the stairs. They kept me awake. Presently I heard the distant strains of carol singers and the groaning of an accompanying bass viol. I ascertained in the morning that the performers were the choir of the Meeting House. The Church, buried in sleep, did not sing to greet the Saviour's birth. The chapel choir itinerated all night till five o'clock in the morning. They visited every house in the parish except those of the parson and the squire, for the former were too orthodox to tolerate dissenting music, and the latter was absent from home. At their return they were all the worse for liquor. In church this morning there were twelve persons, of these nearly all were from the Rectory.

The Drunken Maidens

Sabine Baring-Gould, was a prolific novelist, poet and hymn writer. However, he believed that 'the principal achievement of my life' occurred when he visited over sixty elderly illiterate singers in the region and, with his collaborators, set to music scores of traditional folk songs, such as the now world-famous 'Widecombe Fair'. This work ensured that this rich heritage was saved for ever. Originally published in four volumes between 1889–91, the final revised edition appeared as *Songs of the West* in 1905. The following song is a seasonal variation on a bawdy ballad which appeared in the collection:

There were four drunken maidens,
Went out on New Year's Eve,
They stepped into a tavern,
And without a by your leave,
Supped throughout the night
And would not then go out
Not the four drunken maidens,
As they pushed the jug about.

It was woodcock and pheasant,
And partridge and hare,
It was all kind of dainties,
No scarcity was there,
It was four quarts of Malaga,
Each fairly did drink out,
So the four drunken maidens,
They pushed the jug about.

Sabine Baring-Gould.

Then down came the landlord,
And asked for his pay,
O! a forty-pound bill, Sirs!
The damsels drew that day.
It was ten pounds apiece, Sirs!
But yet, they would not out.
So the four drunken maidens,
They pushed the jug about.

'O where be your spencers?
Your mantles rich and fine?'
'They all be a swallowed
In tankards of good wine'.

'O where be your characters
Ye maidens brisk and gay?'
'O they be a swallowed!
'We've drunk them clean away'.

The Ghost of the Little Giant

The greatest engineer of the Industrial Revolution, Isambard Kingdom Brunel (1806-1859) designed and built some of the world's finest viaducts, bridges, tunnels, ships and railways. Amongst his outstanding achievements was the pioneering vessel *The Great Western* – the first steamship to cross the Atlantic, the architectural splendour of Paddington Railway Station and the elegant Clifton Suspension Bridge spanning the Avon Gorge at Bristol. The charismatic innovator also left his mark in Devon, with the bold experiment of the Atmospheric Engine, the completion of the scenic railroad running along the beautiful coastline of South Devon's holiday resorts and the construction of the Royal Albert Bridge at Saltash, enabling trains to cross the River Tamar.

At the age of twenty-six, Brunel was appointed chief engineer to the newly formed Great Western Railway. By the time he had supervised the construction of the London to Bristol line that opened in 1841, the GWR was well on its way to becoming known as 'God's Wonderful Railway' by steam enthusiasts. After extending the line from Bristol to Exeter, Brunel undertook the building of the South Devon Railway from Exeter to Torquay. For this venture, he attempted to introduce a revolutionary new system – the Atmospheric Engine. Instead of trains being pulled by locomotives, they were propelled by air pressure. Stationary engines, housed in pumping stations, were placed every five kilometres along the track at Exeter, Starcross, Dawlish, Teignmouth, Newton Abbot, Torquay and Totnes. To operate the system, air was sucked along a pipe laid between the tracks that moved the train forward when linked to the leading carriage. Trials took place between Exeter and Teignmouth but ended in a rare failure for Brunel. Running costs escalated when rats found the leather valves

Isambard Kingdom Brunel.

St Marychurch Parish Church.

coated in grease extremely appetising, and the damage they caused resulted in loss of air pressure. Interminable delays to progress resulted in the scheme's financial backers losing confidence in the project. It was eventually abandoned in favour of a conventional railroad – albeit running on Brunel's broad gauge tracks, which would later be standardised in 1892.

Brunel had a strong urge to settle in South Devon. It became a forlorn hope of his to escape the overwhelming pressures of work and retire to the county that meant so much to him, as his mother Sophia Kingdom had been born and raised in Plymouth. During the last ten years of his life, he spent the summers with his family staying in a rented villa at Torquay. He purchased 163 acres of land on the outskirts of the town at Watcombe Park, in the parish of St Marychurch, which he described as 'an estate where all is to be done'. Brunel supervised the building of new roads, planted the bare hillsides with trees and laid out the grounds advised by landscape gardener William Nesfield. The foremost country house architect of the day, William Burn, was commissioned to draw up plans for a mansion and the foundations were laid. Sadly, Brunel did not live to see his dream home completed. A fatal kidney disease was diagnosed and the great man passed away in his prime. His son and namesake, Isambard, testified about his father's love for Watcombe, for it was here 'that the happiest hours of his life were spent'.

Brunel generously supported worthy causes and involved themselves in local affairs. He successfully spoke out on behalf of the neighbourhood to the House of Lords, who agreed to his objections and threw out a proposal to spoil the beauty of Babbacombe Beach by installing a gas works there. Regularly attending St Marychurch Parish Church, Brunel was the largest single contributor to rebuilding work and also made a generous donation to provide a new church organ. Soon after his death there were reported sightings on the streets of Babbacombe and St Marychurch of a small ghostly figure wearing the innovative engineer's trademark 'stovepipe' hat. Furthermore, early in the morning on New Year's Day, a local character in an intoxicated state was walking past the parish church on his way home from the pub, when he spotted the ghost of 'the Little Giant'. The apparition walked up the path towards the church and passed through the closed wooden doors. This strange occurrence was followed by the strains of ethereal music coming from the church organ in the empty church. Running away as fast as his unsteady legs could carry him, the drunk quickly sobered up due to the shock of this terrifying experience. Despite the incredulous reception by his friends to his wild tale, he took the pledge and it was said that he was never tempted to touch another drop as long as he lived!

I Wish You Merry Christmas

By F.W. Matthews from *Tales of the Blackdown Borderland* (1923):

> I wish you merry Christmas and a happy New Year,
> Your pockets full of money and your barrels full of beer,
> So I wish you all a happy New Year, New Year, New Year,
> So I wish you all a happy New Year
>
> Here's a health to you in water, I would it was in wine,
> And all the money you have got, I'm sure it's none of mine,
> So I wish you all a happy New Year, New Year, New Year,
> So I wish you all a happy New Year
>
> Here's a health unto our master and mistress alike,
> And all the pretty family around the fireside,
> So I wish you all a happy New Year, New Year, New Year,
> So I wish you all a happy New Year

'All the pretty family around the fireside'.

The Devil's Punchbowl

Near the summit of Hartland Tor is a cavity known as the Devil's Punchbowl, doubtless where Devon's favourite tipple is prepared by Dewer:

Cider Punch

Take one quart of iced cider, one bottle of iced seltzer or soda-water, one wine glass of brandy, one thinly-sliced lemon, add sugar to taste. Mix all the ingredients together in a glass jug and serve in small glasses.

Hot Tip – Mulled Cider

For a delicious mulled drink pour two pints of dry cider into a pan with four tablespoons of honey, add an orange

peel and spice with one inch cube of grated fresh ginger, two cinnamon sticks, six whole cloves, one star anise. Adjusting spices to taste, heat gently taking care not to boil. Pour into glasses through a sieve then add a generous glug of warm cider brandy to each.

Tipsy Cake

For six servings take eight sponge cakes, raspberry jam, one pint of boiled custard, ¼ pint of sherry. Split the cakes, spread on a good layer of jam, replace the halves, and arrange them compactly in a dish, giving them as far as possible the appearance of one large cake. Pour over the sherry and let them soak for one hour. Make the custard and when cool, pour it over. The cake may be garnished with cherries, angelica, chopped pistachios or baked almonds.

Tipsy Puddings

For six servings take 3oz of flour, 3oz of castor sugar, three eggs, three or four tablespoons of rum, desiccated coconut. Beat the eggs and sugar together until thick and smooth, and stir in the flour as lightly as possible. Coat six or seven well-buttered dariol moulds thickly with castor sugar, fill them three-quarters full with the mixture and bake for fifteen to twenty minutes in a moderately hot oven. When cooked, baste them with fruit syrup, sweetened to taste, sprinkled lightly with coconut, and serve cold.

Hot Tip

As an alternative to fruit syrup, baste the tipsy puddings with lashings of rum.

Waldorf had been born in New York on the same day as Nancy. His father, Viscount William Astor, had not endeared himself to his fellow countrymen when he moved his family to England in 1899, publicly stating, 'America is not a fit place for a gentleman to live'. Becoming a British subject ten years later, he took a short cut to a peerage by becoming a newspaper tycoon.

In 1908, Waldorf entered politics. Refusing the offer of a safe seat, he became the Tory candidate for Plymouth Sutton, attracted by its historical association with the Pilgrim Fathers and America. Two years later, at the second attempt, he won the seat from the Liberals. During the First World War he served as Parliamentary Private Secretary to Prime Minister, David Lloyd George, before his career in the Commons came to an end upon the death of his father in 1919. Waldorf inherited the peerage and was obliged to move to the House of Lords.

The part played by women in British society while men were at war had finally won them the vote and the right to stand for Parliament. Lady Astor became the first successful women candidate when she fought a by-election and won the seat vacated by her husband, which she was to hold for twenty-five years. In her maiden speech she requested, 'I do not want you to look on your lady member as a fanatic or lunatic. I am simply trying to speak for the hundreds of women and children throughout the country who cannot speak for themselves'.

Her plea fell on deaf ears, the 'woman in the house' was mocked relentlessly, her presence bitterly resented in a hitherto exclusive gentleman's club with no facilities for women.

Winston Churchill could not bring himself to speak to her in the Commons for years. When Nancy confronted him about his attitude he replied, 'Well, when you entered the House of Commons I felt as though some woman had entered my bathroom and I had nothing to protect myself with except a sponge.' A controversy ensued when a painting of Nancy's historic entry into Parliament flanked by Lloyd George and Arthur Balfour was removed from the House of Commons following petty protests that it was a dangerous precedent to have a picture portraying living politicians.

Nancy gradually overcame male bias. As a spirited opponent of socialism, a champion of women's rights and children's welfare, she won popularity as one of the most flamboyant personalities in British public life. During the Second World War, Waldorf and Nancy were Lord and Lady Mayor of Plymouth. Firebombs hit their home, Astor House, on the Hoe during the first serious raid of the Blitz. Displaying the bulldog spirit of her adopted country, Lady Astor donned her tin helmet and went up on the roof to inspect the damage. With glass splinters in her hair from the shattered windows, she shouted, 'Where the hell are the buckets of sand for the roof?'

When Nancy retired from politics at the end of the war, the Astors had served the people of Plymouth for thirty-five years. Waldorf died in 1952, having supervised the reconstruction plans for the war-ravaged city. On her eightieth birthday in 1959, Nancy became the only woman to be honoured with the Freedom of Plymouth. She died on 2 May 1964 after a stroke. Her ashes were buried wrapped in a Confederate flag and it appears she continues to be a 'rebel' beyond the grave, haunting Westminster where she was insultingly dismissed by her critics as a 'Yankee at King Arthur's court'.

Sir John Barleycorn

This amusing tale at the expense of the temperance movement was published by Sabine Baring-Gould in *Songs of the West* (1905). The story personalises the source of beer as 'John Barleycorn' and all efforts to kill him off only result in the production of more alcohol:

> There came three men from out the West
> Their victory to try;
> And they have taken a solemn oath,
> Poor Barleycorn must die.
>
> They took a plough and ploughed him in,
> Clods harrowed on his head;
> And then they took a solemn oath
> John Barleycorn was dead.
>
> There he lay sleeping in the ground
> Till rain on him did fall;
> Then Barleycorn sprung up his head
> And so amazed them all.
>
> There he remained till Midsummer
> And look'd both pale and wan;

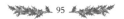

Travelling musicians at Christmas.

Then Barleycorn he got a beard
And so became a man.

Then they sent men with scythes so sharp
To cut him off at the knee;
And then poor Johnny Barleycorn
They served most barbarously.

Then they sent men with pitch forks strong
To pierce him through the heart;
And like a doleful Tragedy
They bound him in a cart.

And then they brought him to a barn
A prisoner to endure;
And so they fetched him out again
And laid him on the floor.

Then they set men with holly clubs
To beat the flesh from th' bones;
But the miller served him worse than that
He ground him 'twixt two stones.

O! Barleycorn is the choicest grain
That 'ere was sown on land;
And it will cause a man to drink
Till he neither can go nor stand.

It will make a boy into a man
A man into a ass;
To silver it will change your gold
Your silver into brass.

three

CHRISTMAS TIME –
MYSTERY AND CRIME

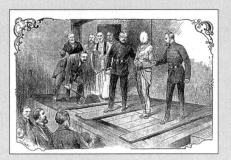

Christmas 'Time' on Dartmoor

These are the stories of two seasonal escapes from Dartmoor Prison and the tragic consequences for prisoners Frank 'Madman' Mitchell and William Carter:

Dartmoor Prison attracted lurid headlines when Frank 'Mad Axeman' Mitchell escaped from a working party at Peter Tavy, five miles from Tavistock. The violent former Broadmoor and Rampton patient had previously escaped from both institutions and once, whilst on the run, had robbed an elderly couple in their home after threatening them with an axe, earning himself the sobriquet 'the Mad Axeman'. For this crime he was sentenced to life imprisonment for robbery with violence, with no fixed date for his release.

There was a national outcry when it was learned that such a dangerous career-criminal was not incarcerated in a high-security prison. Furthermore, it transpired that the prisoner had been able to wander away unnoticed from work parties and roam the moor, where he had been known to regularly enjoy the hospitality of village pubs. Following Mitchell's escape on Monday 12 December 1966, one of the greatest manhunts in Dartmoor's history was mounted. Moorland farmers were warned to lock their properties securely and the public were instructed not to approach the fugitive. A senior police officer said, 'He is a dangerous man who will stop at nothing. He is not to be trifled with.'

However, local people had nothing to fear as it was later learned that Mitchell had been whisked away by car to

Escape on Dartmoor.

London by members of the infamous Kray gang. National newspapers received letters from Mitchell offering to give himself up if he was given hope of freedom, 'The reason for my absence from Dartmoor was to bring to the notice of my unhappy plight, to be truthful I am asking for a possible date of release'. The Home Secretary could not bow to such demands and 'Big Frank' was never recaptured.

His fate was shrouded in mystery until the notorious Kray brothers were brought to trial for their criminal activities in 1969. It was alleged that Mitchell had been killed on 23 December 1966 after becoming demanding and troublesome while cooped up in a London flat. The gangland brothers were cleared of the charge but it was later revealed by criminal sources that three of their henchmen had taken Mitchell to a van on the pretext that he was going to spend Christmas with Ronnie Kray in Kent. After a violent struggle, he was shot dead, although it took twelve bullets to finish him off. An unsubstantiated rumour persists that his corpse was then disposed of in a concrete mixer and poured into a pillar supporting a motorway bridge.

Before motor vehicles came into general use, Dartmoor prisoners on the run had many obstacles to overcome – the grim weather, swirling mists that could envelop the landscape and reduce visibility to zero in seconds, treacherous bogs where many 'successful' escapees may have been sucked and sharp-eyed local people known as 'five-pounders', eager to claim a £5 reward for apprehending a fleeing villain. Fugitives also risked death at the hands of their pursuers. The irony of the law of the land which protected game birds, yet justified a shoot-on-sight policy against convicts in flight, was not lost on 'An Old Dartmoor Lag' who humorously illustrated the point in a poem, *The Lay of the Lagged Minstrel*, composed in 1907:

> Sometimes when things are very dull, a convict makes a dash
> To gain his freedom, but the guards of him soon make a hash
> Lag-shooting is such a good old sport it's never out of season,
> But to shoot a pheasant in July is almost worse than treason.

One such tragedy occurred at 11 a.m. on Christmas Eve 1896, when three men made a run from a work party digging peat near the Blackabrook River. The chief instigator was twenty-two-year-old William Carter, who had been recently parted from his new bride to serve a twelve-year sentence for robbery with violence. His co-conspirators were Ralph Goodwin and John Martin, both serving long sentences for burglary. As the mist descended and visibility deteriorated rapidly, work was abandoned and the armed escort ordered the party to march back to the prison. On a signal from Carter, earth was thrown into the faces of the guards and the trio dashed for the cover of some woodland. The fleeing Carter was cut down by a hail of bullets and died instantly, while Martin was quickly cornered and knocked cold with a truncheon. Meanwhile, Goodwin vanished into the mist and spent the rest of the day trying to put as much distance as possible between himself and Princetown. As dawn broke the tired and hungry convict was dismayed to discover that he had travelled in a complete circle and arrived back within sight of the prison. Tempted to give himself up but worried he might meet the same fate as Carter, he set out again and made good progress on Christmas Day. At one point he was spotted by a distant search party and gave them a cheeky wave of his hat before disappearing from view. That night he broke into two houses at Postbridge and obtained a change of clothes. On Boxing Day, he reached Tavistock and raided another house and hungrily ate the remains of a Christmas dinner before spending the night trudging along the railway track towards Plymouth. By morning he had reached Devonport. With a successful getaway within his grasp, he took to the streets where his escapade immediately came to an end due to a guilt complex. He met a policeman and wished him 'Good morning' without arousing suspicion, then, when the policeman's dog ran playfully after him, he believed he had been rumbled, lost his nerve and ran off. The exhausted fugitive was chased by the officer and quickly cornered, then flashed a stolen knife at his pursuer. The policeman calmly out-bluffed his assailant by pretending he had a gun, which he threatened he would have no hesitation in using unless the desperate criminal gave himself up. Returning to Dartmoor, where any vestige of festive spirit had been quashed by the death of a fellow inmate, Goodwin and Martin subsequently gave evidence at the inquest of William Carter, whose untimely death, caused by thirteen bullet wounds in the back, was pronounced 'justifiable homicide'.

The Christmas Sale

In Plymouth and Devonport, in *Times of War and Peace* (1900), author H.F. Whitfield recounted an extraordinary incident where a man was arrested for auctioning his wife:

In December 1822 the town crier of Plymouth announced that James Brooks intended to dispose of his spouse by public auction. The lady was advertised as young and handsome, and as being likely to succeed to an inheritance of £700. Expectation was whetted by the intimation that she meant to attend the sale of her own free will, and to ride to market on horseback. A curious and babbling crowd assembled to behold 'the marvel'. At precisely midday, in accordance with the announcement, she rode up, attended by the ostler of the Lord Exmouth. The husband offici-ated as the auctioneer; and, from 5s, the bidding advanced to 10s and then 15s. As the competition grew keen on the part of the onlookers, £3 was offered by the ostler. At this point two watchmen interposed, one laying hands on wife and another on husband, and the ill-matched pair were escorted to the Guildhall. When the mayor took them to task, the husband vowed that he did not think they were doing wrong. He and his wife agreed to the sale, as they had not lived together for a long time. She was not faithful to him, since she had cohabited with others; and as the ostler was prepared to pay £20 for her – £3 down and the balance at Christmas – and the woman was quite agreeable, he could not perceive that he had erred. There was nothing 'below board' in the transaction, the auction had been 'called' three times in Modbury market and the wife also thought that she could be sold at a public fair. The mayor asked the name of the individual who had agreed to buy her. 'Mr K.', said she, 'and I am very much annoyed to find that he has not kept his promise. But I was so determined to be loosed from Mr Brooks that, when Mr K. did not attend, I asked the ostler to buy me with my own money, unless I went for more than £20'. Taking into consideration the ignorance of the parties, the justices bound them over in sureties to be of good behaviour.

The Man They Could Not Hang

The Christmas edition of *Lloyd's Weekly News* in 1907 published a sworn affidavit by a newly-released prisoner, John Lee, denying any involvement in the murder for which he had been condemned to death before mysteriously surviving three execution attempts.

After serving twenty-three years in prison, convicted murderer John 'Babbacombe' Lee was released in time to spend the festive season with his aged mother at the family home in Abbotskerswell. Despite his pleas of innocence, the infamous manservant had been arrested in November 1884, charged with the gruesome murder of his elderly employer, Emma Keyse, at her home, the Glen, on Babbacombe Beach, Torquay. Robbery had not been committed and there was no sign of a forced entry. Therefore, suspicion fell upon the only male among the four servants present in the house – John Lee.

Tried at Exeter Castle in February 1885, he was sentenced to hang. He then incredibly escaped execution when the trapdoors of the scaffold mysteriously failed to open on three occasions when the prisoner stepped onto the platform. This fuelled the legend of 'the Man They Could Not Hang'. Mortified officials abandoned the execution and the death penalty was commuted to life imprisonment following the intervention of Queen Victoria, who sent the following telegram to the Home Secretary, 'I am horrified at the disgraceful scenes at Exeter at Lee's execution. Surely Lee cannot be executed. It would be too cruel. Imprisonment for life seems the

FINDING THE BODY OF MISS KEYSE

only alternative'. The Home Secretary concurred and told a packed House of Commons, 'It would shock the feelings of everyone if a man twice had to pay the pangs of imminent death.'

At the time of John Lee's deliverance, when he became the only man in British legal history to survive the method of execution known as the 'long drop', there was speculation that he had been saved by either an act of God or the work of the Devil. In stark contrast to the prosecution's portrayal of a depraved lunatic capable of smashing an old lady's head with an axe, then slashing her throat with a knife before setting fire to the lifeless body, the judge, in passing sentence of death, remarked how calm the demeanour of the accused had been throughout the trial. The prisoner leaned forward in the dock and replied firmly, 'The reason why I am so calm is that I trust in the Lord, and He knows I am innocent'. In the days leading up to the date of execution, Lee read the Bible prodigiously and intimated to the prison chaplain that the real culprit was the lover of his half-sister, Elizabeth Harris, who was cook at the Glen and expecting a child, later delivered in Newton Abbot workhouse. Following his reprieve, Lee announced his belief that he had been saved by divine intervention and on the morning of the execution, told two prison guards that he had dreamt that, 'Three times the bolt was drawn, and three times the bolt failed to act'. As Lee predicted, between each of the three attempts the trapdoors were tested and opened normally, but refused to budge as soon as he stood upon them. It was also rumoured that throughout the ordeal on the scaffold, a white dove perched on the gallows until the condemned man was led safely back to his prison cell.

Contradicting this view, friends of Lee claimed they had handsomely paid a white witch to save him from the noose. Country folk told stories of how John Lee's mother had visited the church graveyard near her home at Abbotskerswell, recited the Lord's Prayer backwards and summoned the Evil One to save her son, whilst Granny Lee of Ogwell told locals, 'They shall not hang him' as she walked to Exeter on the morning of the execution and cast a spell on the gallows from a spot overlooking

THE BABBICOMBE MURDER- SHOCKING SCENES on the SCAFFOLD

the prison. In 1905, the witchcraft theory gained credence from a surprising source – the Archdeacon of Westminster, Basil Wilberforce. At the time of the murder he had been a regular visitor to Babbacombe where he addressed temperance meetings organised by a distinguished neighbour of Emma Keyse, Lady Mount-Temple of Babbacombe Cliff. The churchman was chaplain to the House of Commons and vehemently opposed a growing campaign for Lee's release, informing the Home Office that he 'knew the Lees well' and they were 'a well-known witch family on Dartmoor'.

A Living Hell

Within hours of his release, 'the Man They Could Not Hang' sold his exclusive story to *Lloyd's Weekly News* and described his prison sentence as a 'living Hell'. He high-lighted the fact that inmates were fed inadequate rations that were occasionally supplemented at special times like Christmas with oranges or figs paid for from the meagre earnings received in return for 'hard labour'. The criminal celebrity passed on the following unappetising culinary tips to readers about to prepare their Christmas dinner:

In the old days, when I first went to prison, we did not get so much food as they do now. Then they used to keep you practically in a starving condition. To a certain extent that has been altered. You get plenty of food now but half of it is uneatable. ...Prison is not supposed to be a place of luxury, but the food should be eatable. ... For seventeen years I only had dry bread at breakfast and cocoa for supper. Only once in nineteen years did I taste vegetables. But now vegetables are served out twice a week, and a man gets one half of an ounce of butter at breakfast.

Think of the suffering all this entailed to me, brought up as I was in Devonshire, a county that abounds in good things; a county in which beautiful rich cream finds a place on even the humblest of tables. ... But I must not grumble. Let me show you something that should be interesting to every housewife, to every man who is accustomed to a good home and to good cooking. Here are the official recipes for prison food:

BREAD - To be made with wholemeal flour, consisting of all the products of the wheaten grain, with the exception of 12% of coarse bran and coarse pollards.

GRUEL-To every pint 2ozs coarse Scotch oatmeal, ½oz sugar.

COCOA - To every pint ¾oz Admiralty cocoa, 2ozs milk, ¾oz sugar.

SUET PUDDING - To every lb. 2oz beef suet, 8ozs white or whole-meal flour.

VEGETABLE SOUP - To every pint, clod or shoulder, leg or shin of beef in the proportion of 8ozs and, in addition, the soup to contain 1oz pearl barley, 2ozs fresh vegetables, 1oz onions, ¼oz flour, with pepper and salt.

MEAT LIQOUR - The allowance of cooked mutton or beef to be served with its own liquor, flavoured with ½oz onions, and thickened with ⅛oz flour, with pepper and salt.

BEANS - Haricot beans or broad or Winsor beans, dried in the green state and decorticated.

Devonshire Cream

The traditional method of producing 'clotted' or 'clouted' cream, sorely missed by John Lee during his period of imprisonment, was described by J.M. Hawker in a paper submitted to the Devonshire Association in 1881:

> The manner of producing clouted cream is as follows: The milk is strained into shallow pans, each containing about half-a-pint of water to prevent the milk from adhering to the sides. In these it is allowed to remain undisturbed for twelve or twenty-four hours, according to the weather. It is then scalded, and often in Devonshire farmhouses by a wood fire (which gives the butter made from it the smoky taste that some like and some dislike), or better, according to modern usage, by warm water. In the former case it is moved slowly towards the fire so as to become gradually heated, and in about forty or fifty minutes the cream is formed. This is indicated by bubbles, and takes the place at a temperature of 180 degrees Fahrenheit. The milk is then removed from the fire, and skimmed from twelve to thirty-six hours afterwards.

Jack the Ripper in Devon

How an actor who later became a suspect in the Whitechapel Murders made a surprise appearance in the world premier of a classic Gilbert and Sullivan comic opera at Paignton:

Scenes from *The Pirates of Penzance* during its first showing in London.

The pantomime season took a bizarre twist at Paignton in 1879. On 29 December, at the aptly named Bijou Theatre, an audience of only seventy people witnessed the farcical world premier of *The Pirates of Penzance*. The celebrated composers Gilbert and Sullivan secretly arranged the performance to protect their copyright. Members of the Doyle Carte Company appearing in HMS *Pinafore* at the nearby town of Torquay, were hastily summoned for a bizarre one-off rendition of the new work, reading and singing from their scripts while dressed in their *Pinafore* costumes. Hurriedly creating the soon-to-be coveted role of the Major-General was actor Richard Mansfield, who

Richard Mansfield as
Dr Jekyll and
Mr Hyde.

nine years later found himself starring as Dr Jekyll and
Mr Hyde in London's West End while serial killer Jack
the Ripper was making a name for himself in the East
End. During the run-up to Christmas in 1888, rumours
circulated connecting Richard Mansfield to the crimes.
Scotland Yard was swamped with letters naming suspects from members of the public, including several from
disturbed theatre-goers who were tormented by the har-
rowing performance they had witnessed and could not
believe that an actor could be so convincing in a stage role
without being a murderer in real life. They alleged that he
must be Jack the Ripper.

The Kenton Ghost

The poetical saga of a petty thief written by 'Tickler' (probably the pseudonym of a journalist) which appeared in the festive edition of the *Devon Weekly Times* in 1864:

In order, first, to launch by rhyme,
Know, friends, that 'once upon a time'
A ghost appear'd in Kenton town,
Which lieth south, some sev'n miles down
From Exon, where one Tuckett dwelt,
Who could e'en ghosts to nothing melt;
And at whose wink, or nod, or cough,
Sir Lucifer would 'missle' off;
Or, perhaps, the plainer words to put,
The very Devil himself would cut.

But, first of all to clear the case,
Let me in brief describe the place:
The main part is a straggling street
(no matter as to yards or feet),
And half of which, it will be found,
Compriseth parish burial ground,
Where, villagers can swear by hosts,
They've heard and witness'd 'rayal' ghosts.
But I'm running on in measure wild,
And my gentle muse saith – draw it mild,
Methinks you will have got to glory,
Before you reach your promised story,
Dear muse allows me just to say,

You meeting trouble are half way,
But as you're in a hurried way,
I'll tell the tale of Fanny Bray,
Promising (for its much the same)
'Tis only an adopted name.
Old Fanny was a quiet soul,
Who burnt up wood instead of coal –
Because the one was got for 'nort'
The other, as she said, was 'bort'
So of the two she'd rather fix
Upon the course of picking sticks.
Time was when gentlefolk would give
The poor around a chance to live
Thro' winter, free from legal harm
For picking sticks to keep them warm,
Until the county bobbies came,
And made the sticks as scarce as game,
'Hood picking' in the good old time,
Was honest, but now 'tis crime,
I heard a poor 'hoodpicker' say,
Who'd to the prison found his way,
Because he had taken to himself
Some twopence worth of wooden pelf.
No doubt such a law will come in soon
To send such culprits to the moon;
Where one poor chap, for years untold,
Hath in that distant planet rolled
For having, when 'twas cold and windy,
Pick'd up a stick or two on 'Zunday'.
All I can say's – I'd have a clause

Christmas crime - 'Quick, run for it!'

If such e'er be among our laws:
To make each prosecutor pace
Straight to the moon, to prove his case;
And in such trivial offences
Just make him pay his own expenses.
But I'm digressing, you will say,
'And what about old Fanny Bray?'
Well, Fanny wasn't to be done,
And had for many years been one,
To ramble where she cared or could,
Her object being 'picking hood'.
The bobbies knew her, but 'No go'.
She'd smell 'em for a mile or so.
And thus for years her sticks she scap'd,
And from their tender mercies 'scaped.

'Twas said her escapades were 'sich'
That Fanny Bray must be a witch;
And, being such a weird old crony,
Must be, of course, possess'd of money,
But there's a 'bobby' who, one day,
Laid his strong hand on Fanny Bray,
This 'bobby' wasn't dress'd in blue,
With buttons running all down through;
He had no cudgel in his hand
With which to make offenders 'stand';
His face was measured, firm yet slow,
His lightest touch a knock-down blow;
Paralysis was in his breath,
This bobby's name, my friends was 'Death'.
In silence he'd around her gone,
She never heard him say 'move on'.
And thus it is, from day to day,
We live on in careless way;
By our own heedlessness defended,
Until at last we're apprehended:
'Twas for this self-same heedless way
The Peeler Death took Fanny Bray;
For this she got into a fix,
But not for picking a few sticks.
What was it then's the question giv'n
That kept poor Fan from going to Heaven;
For she was seen, or else folk lied,
In her old house the night she died;
And at her window every night,
For weeks appear'd in lurid light,

At twelve o'clock, as 'safe's a gun',
And sometimes quite as late as one,
She at her window would appear,
As if just risen from the bier;
And there she'd stay some half the night,
Till all was at once she'd flash away,
Perhaps she feared the approach of day.
Jan Morrish, with his night-cap on,
Look'd in the room, and 'smul'd a smul'
And for weeks after 'wad'n wul'
And, when he came out from the dark,
Upon his night-cap was a mark,
'Ya niver', said he, 'zeed the fella
Awt: 'twas Brimstone cuz 'twizz yeller'.
Well, soon the news got spread abroad,
And every night the middle road
Was thronged by such an eager host
Of folks to see the Kenton Ghost.
A local preacher had 'a pray'
To drive poor Fanny's ghost away;
But not a bit of use was that –
In spite of all still there she sat.
'Twas said, 'Hur wid'n laive her perch,
Cuz the parson waren't in the church'.
One day the daughter of poor Fan
To Exon came to see the man,
Who, of all others, knew the way,
'Twas said a 'thousand ghosts to lay'.
The learned man was surnam'd Tuckett,
And once had found Fan's 'darter's bucket'.

He gave her sev'ral little stones,
Tied in a bab, and said Fan's bones
Would knock against her coffin lid,
That 'if so be' her 'darter' did
Say 'picky, wicky, rum tum, tee'
Twice for each stone – no harm in three.
The spirit then would hear the bones,
And after giving several groans,
Her form would then like smoke be curl'd,
And straight be off for t'other world.
She paid the wise man, home she came,
And tried that night her 'little game';
And as she finished 'rum, um, tee',
A lot of folks as well as she
Heard old Fan's voice cry out aloud,
And saw her form roll like a cloud
Away; and never since that night
Have people seen that fearful sight.
Some said the moon, with curious light,
Was in the window 'shining bright'
And there were other folks that vow'd
'Twas nothing but a passing cloud
That, with a slow and solemn pace,
Was floating 'near her moonship's face.

A Twist in the Plot

This is the story of how the world's most popular crime novelist became the central character in a real-life mystery:

The atmosphere in the Christie household on Christmas Eve 1926 must have been distinctly 'frosty'. For although it was Agatha and Archie's twelfth wedding anniversary, the marriage was heading for divorce. Earlier in the month their strained relationship had led to a nationwide hunt when Agatha drove off late at night on Friday 3 December – leaving behind her wedding ring at the marital home in Sunningdale, Berkshire. The 'Queen of Crime' left a further trail of clues that Hercule Poirot or Miss Marples would doubtless have solved easily, but the police took longer to interpret the evidence. On Saturday morning Agatha's Morris Cowley car was found abandoned at Newlands Corner, Shere, Surrey. Beside a nearby tree, concealed in a shaving tin, was a cryptic note naming two men. 'Ask X', it said, naming one of them. 'He knows more about the Silent Pool than Y'. The pool was located a quarter of a mile away and according to local folklore a young woman had drowned there in medieval times whilst bathing and swimming out of her depth to avoid the lustful advances of King John. The Silent Pool was dragged to no avail, but hopes for the author's safety were raised when Archie's brother received a postcard from Agatha saying that she was travelling to an unspecified spa town in Yorkshire. It had been posted on Saturday a few hours after her car had been discovered on the Surrey Downs. When inquiries in

Agatha Christie.

Yorkshire came to naught, the police in Torquay became involved when they visited the author's birthplace, Ashfield. The house was found to be derelict following the death of Agatha's mother six months earlier.

The press began to suspect that the whole thing was a publicity stunt to promote her books. The police investigation was held up by Archie, who was naturally reluctant to reveal that the couple had argued on the day of his wife's departure. He had admitted to her that he was having an affair, before leaving the house to spend the weekend with his lover. The police interviewed the Christie's servants and learned of the couple's domestic problems. Archie immediately became suspected of murder and a week later the pressure was clearly getting to him when he spoke to the *Evening News*:

I cannot account for her disappearance save that her nerves have completely gone, and that she went away for no real purpose whatever. I left home on Friday to spend the weekend with friends. Where I stayed I am not prepared to state. I have told the police. I do not want my friends to be dragged into this. It is my business alone. I have been badgered and pestered like a criminal, and all I want is to be left alone. My telephone is constantly ringing. All manner of people are asking about my wife. Why, I even get clairvoyants ringing me up and telling me the only hope of finding her is by holding a séance.

Sir Arthur Conan Doyle, the creator of Sherlock Holmes, did not use the deductive powers of his fictional detective but utilised the services of medium Horace Leaf. He handed him a glove belonging to the missing writer. 'I gave him no clue at all as to what I wanted or to whom the article belonged,' Sir Arthur later recalled, 'he never saw it until I laid it on the table at the moment of consultation, and there was nothing to connect either it or me with the Christie case... He at once got the name Agatha. "There is trouble connected with this article. The person who owns it is half-dazed and half-purposeful. She is not dead as many think. She is alive. You will hear of her next Wednesday"'.

Indeed, the world did learn of Agatha's whereabouts the following Wednesday when newspapers broke the news that she had been found staying at a luxury hotel in Harrogate. As the only person in the ballroom not wearing evening dress, Agatha had not been hard to recognise by members of the orchestra as she danced in front of the

BERKSHIRE CONSTABULARY,
WOKINGHAM DIVISION.

9th. December 1926

MISSING

From her home "Styles" Sunningdale in this Division.

Mrs. Agatha Mary Clarissa CHRISTIE

(WIFE OF COLONEL A. CHRISTIE)

AGE 35 YEARS, HEIGHT 5 ft. 7 ins., HAIR RED (Shingled), NATURAL
TEETH, EYES GREY, COMPLEXION FAIR, WELL BUILT.

DRESSED—Grey Stockingette Skirt, Green Jumper,
Grey and dark Grey Cardigan, small Green Velour Hat,
may have hand bag containing £5 to £10.   Left home in
4 seater Morris Cowley car at 9.45 p.m. on 3rd. December
leaving note saying she was going for a drive.   The next
morning the car was found abandoned at Newlands
Corner, Albury, Surrey.

Should this lady be seen or any information regarding her
be obtained please communicate to any Police Station, or to

CHARLES GODDARD, Superintendent,
WOKINGHAM.

Telephone No. 11 Wokingham.

PRINTED AT THE "BERKSHIRE GAZETTE" OFFICES, PEACH STREET, WOKINGHAM.

bandstand to the tune 'Yes, We Have No Bananas'. Archie was informed, and confronted Agatha in the lounge as she picked up a newspaper bearing her pictures. Next day, the *Western Morning News* reported the reunion, 'There was instant recognition... She seemed to regard him as an acquaintance whose identity she could not quite fix'. Archie Christie proffered an explanation to waiting reporters, 'She is suffering from complete loss of memory and does not know who she is'. Fifty years later Agatha went to her grave without shedding any light on the matter in an autobiography published after her death. Whether she hoped that Archie would miss her and end his affair or simply wanted to ruin his romantic weekend and make him suffer embarrassment at the hands of the police is not clear. Yet, whilst mentioning that she did not wish to dwell on the events that had brought about 'sorrow, despair and heartbreak', she was apparently able to recall the unwanted attention of the press despite claiming to be suffering from amnesia. 'I had felt like a fox, hunted, my earths dug up and yelping hounds following me everywhere...' More evidence of how selective a spurned woman's memory can be was brought home forcibly to Archie Christie when he discovered that his distressed wife had taken refuge in the hotel using an alias – the surname of his mistress!

A Christmas Carol

The poems of Samuel Taylor Coleridge (1852) featured this carol written in 1799 by Ottery St Mary's notable writer in which, 'the Prince of Peace' is born to battle 'the murderous fiend' – war!

The shepherds went their hasty way,
And found the lowly stable shed
Where the Virgin Mary lay:
And now they checked their eager tread,
For to the Babe, that at her bosom clung
A mother's song the Virgin Mother sung.

They told her how a glorious light,
Streaming from a heavenly throng,
Around them shone, suspending night!
While sweeter than a mother's song,
Blest Angels heralded the Saviour's birth,
Glory to God on high! And Peace on Earth.

She listened to the tale divine,
And closer still the babe she prest;
And while she cried, the babe is mine!
The milk rushed faster to her breast:
Joy rose, within her, like a summer's morn;
Peace, Peace on Earth! The Prince of Peace is born.

Thou mother of the Prince of Peace,
Poor, simple and of low estate!

Samuel Taylor Coleridge.

That strife should vanish, battle cease,
O why should this thy soul elate?
Sweet music's loudest note, the poet's story –
Didst thou ne'er love to hear of fame and glory?

And is not War a youthful king
A stately hero clad in mail?
Beneath his footsteps laurels spring:
Him Earth's majesty monarch's hail
Their friend, their playmate! And his bold bright eye
Compels the maiden's love-confessing sigh.

Tell this in some more courtly scene,
To maids and youths in robes of state!
I am a woman poor and mean,

And therefore is my soul elate.
War is a ruffian, all with guilt defiled,
That from their aged father tears his child!

A murderous fiend, by friends adored,
He kills the sire and starves the son;
The husband kills, and from her board
Steals all his widow's toil had won;
Plunder's God's world of beauty; rends away
All safety from the night, all comfort from the day.

Then wisely is my soul elate
That strife should vanish, battle cease;
I'm poor and of low estate,
The Mother of the Prince of Peace,
Joy rises in me, like a summer morn:
Peace, Peace on Earth! The Prince of Peace is born.

The Great Pearl Mystery

This is the true story of one of the great society scandals of
the Victorian age:

A sensational society scandal involving an allegation of
slander over the strange disappearance of some pearl pen-
dants came to a dramatic conclusion in the Royal Courts
of Justice in London. Three days before Christmas 1891,
the judge, Mr Justice Denham, announced that he had
received a letter which may have a significant bearing on

the case. Therefore, the court was adjourned until the following day.

Earlier, in February of that year, Georgiana Hargreve discovered that some of her jewellery had disappeared from a secret drawer at her villa, 'Shirley', in Torquay. The trick of opening the drawer of the cabinet was known only to Mrs Hargreve; her husband, retired Army officer Major George Hargreve, who at the time was in poor health and abroad at the health spa Aix; Mr Engelhart, a neighbour and friend of the family; and finally, a recent visitor to her home, her cousin, Miss Ethel Elliot, who resided in London.

Although the owner of the pearls could not bear to suspect her young relative, who was about to enter into matrimony with Captain Arthur Osborne of the Dragoon Guards, Mr Engelhart offered to make some discreet inquiries. Journeying to the capital, he quickly located the missing gems in a jewellery shop owned by John Spink. He learned that they had been acquired on 19 February from a lady, who received a crossed cheque for £550 before returning four days later to exchange it for an open cheque. When shown two or three photographs of the suspect by Mr Engelhart, the jeweller confirmed that Miss Elliott was indeed the lady in question, although she had not used that name. Proceeding to the jeweller's bank, Mr Engelhart discovered that the cheque had been cashed for gold and the young lady had gone off with her ill-gotten gains in a canvas bag. Once again, the photographs of Miss Elliott suggested to the clerks the general appearance of the fair filibuster.

The amateur sleuth communicated his painful findings to Miss Elliott's brother, who in turn broke the bad news to Captain Osborne. When he approached his fiancée with the allegations, Miss Elliott demanded to be confronted with her accusers at the jewellers and the bank. She swore that on 19 February she was not within two miles of these places of business, but was otherwise engaged in choosing her trousseau in South Kensington. Despite her protestations of innocence, Mr Spink and his assistant, after some hesitation, identified her as the woman who sold the pearls and the clerks at the bank did likewise. Firmly believing his betrothed's alibi, Captain Osborne chivalrously went ahead with the marriage on 5 April. He then supported his wife's decision to sue the Hargreves, claiming damages for slander, after the defendants had carelessly confirmed their suspicions in conversations with mutual friends.

When the case came to court in November, the plaintiff was expecting a child, and won much public sympathy for her situation. There was almost universal belief in her innocence, for no one could understand why an independent woman, with inherited wealth and a generous allowance from her family, should feel the need to steal valuables from a cousin who was also her dearest friend. In the witness box, Mrs Osborne apportioned blame to the defendants, claiming Major Hargreve was in the habit of saying that there was no crime he would not commit for 'oof' [slang for 'cash']. In addition, he was mean and his wife often complained he left her short of money. Perhaps this situation had caused Mrs Hargreve herself to dispose of the pearls, for it was a fact, that in the recent past, she had 'lost' another piece of jewellery which had never been recovered.

The 'Torquay Pearl Robbery' was finally solved when the court reconvened after the mysterious adjournment. In a sensational development, counsel for the plaintiff, Sir Charles Russell, rose and stated that he was withdrawing from the case and, under personal instruction from Captain Osborne, unreservedly withdrew the unfounded allegations against the defendants. The letter received by the judge had been sent by a tailor who had cashed the banker's cheque for the culprit. Subsequently one of the £50 notes he had exchanged was traced and found to be endorsed for a purchase by none other than 'Ethel Elliott'. Immediately, a warrant was issued for obtaining a cheque under false

MRS OSBORNE'S REFLECTIONS IN HER GLOOMY CELL.

pretences and perjury, although the thief avoided arrest by immediately packing several large portmanteaus and fleeing to France. At the end of February 1892, the fugitive voluntarily returned, accompanied by her loyal husband, who had shamefacedly resigned his commission, and a detective inspector from Scotland Yard. Ten days later, after being committed for trial at Bow Street magistrates court, Ethel Osbourne (formerly Elliott) pleaded guilty to the charges at the Old Bailey. Then as sentence was about to be passed, the proceedings were remarkably interrupted by her wronged cousin, Georgiana Hargreve, who made a heartfelt plea for mercy on behalf of the sobbing accused. 'I have known her and loved her all my life, and am perfectly convinced she was not in her right mind when she took the jewels'.

Although a sentence of up to seven years imprisonment was deemed appropriate, the judge, mindful of the disgrace she had suffered and her forthcoming confinement, ordered that the defendant serve nine months 'hard labour'. In the event, Mrs Osborne was not required to give birth to her baby in prison as she was released within two months. Most of her sentence was spent in the medical wing of Holloway Prison and her lenient treatment was hastened by an article in the *British Medical Journal* that noted she had been previously treated for hysteria–epilepsy, a condition where 'there is much disturbance of the mental faculties' leading to 'irregular behaviour' which accounted for her irrational criminal activity. The *Western Daily Mercury*, commenting on the incredulity of the case, commented that, 'The whole narrative reads like one of those compendious works of fiction more especially adapted to beguile a single railway journey, and the solution of the mystery has certainly been as artfully concealed from popular penetration'.

The Great Western Railway Robbery

This is the story of the very first robbery from a moving train, planned in Devon:

On New Year's Day 1849, an audacious robbery took place on the 6.35 p.m. Plymouth to London mail train. The perpetrators of the crime, Henry Poole and Edward Nightingale, boarded a first-class carriage and during the journey between Exeter and Bristol gained entry to the unguarded mail van and helped themselves to property valued at over £150,000 which was disposed of and never recovered. The crooks then impudently attempted a repeat performance on the return journey. The mail sacks were found to have been tampered with at Bridgewater and following a search of the train, incriminating evidence was discovered. The pair were then arrested on suspicion and detained at Exeter. The case attracted national interest and featured a banner headline in the *Times*, 'Extraordinary Robbery On The Great Western Railway'.

Edward Nightingale was 'wanted' for another undisclosed crime and refused to give his name. He was not identified until the commencement of the magistrates hearing at Exeter Guildhall, when Detective-Sergeant Edward Langley of Scotland Yard appeared in court and confirmed that the defendant was a 'horse dealer' from Hoxton, London, and well-known to the police. Nine months before the robbery, Henry Poole had inherited a fortune and resigned from his job as a GWR guard.

The London to Plymouth train passing through Dawlish, *c.* 1849.

According to the *Exeter Gazette* he took an elegant residence in Exeter with twenty 'superbly furnished' rooms equipped with furniture 'fit for the mansion of any nobleman'. Despite his wealthy lifestyle, Poole could not resist the lure of easy money and gambled his liberty for a treasure trove.

Donning false moustaches and unfamiliar garb – Nightingale wearing a reversible coat of contrasting colours and Poole, a cloak with a high collar and a green felt broad-rimmed hat – the felons put their plan into action at Starcross. After having a drink at the Courtenay Arms they bought one-way tickets at the station and boarded the night train, seating themselves in one of the private compartments of Brunel's spacious broad gauge first-class carriage behind the mail tender. Poole knew from experience that while the train was travelling between Exeter and Bristol, the guard left the mail van unattended to assist the clerks in the sorting of letters on the adjoining Travelling Post Office. With no stop between Bridgewater and Bristol, there was a window of opportunity allowing the thieves a little over one hour to make their way precariously along the footboards on the outside of the train, using a hook to secure a hold on the top of the carriage, then enter the mail van and plunder the sealed bags containing registered letters and bankers' parcels. The heist was a complete success and they disposed of their plunder to the keeping of unknown accomplices at Bristol, then shortly after midnight calmly purchased tickets for the return journey with a plan to carry out another daring robbery – greed which was to prove their downfall. At Bridgewater, vigilant guards, alerted by news of the earlier loss, made the discovery that mailbags had been rifled. They informed Superintendent Joseph Gibbons of Plymouth, who happened to be travelling on the train as a normal passenger. Realising that the thieves must still be on-board the train, the police officer ordered a search of the carriages at Taunton. Poole and Nightingale, seated suspiciously with the blinds drawn in a compartment of the first-class carriage, were quickly rumbled when a dozen packages were found under their seats wrapped in a shawl, together with false moustaches, crepe masks, hook, string, candle and sealing wax. When questioned about the booty both men replied, 'We know nothing about it'.

The thieves returned to Exeter, not as rich men, but prisoners. The trial commenced at the Spring Assizes held at Exeter Castle. The prosecution had insufficient evidence to connect Poole and Nightingale with the 'up' train robbery, from which valuables were missing, estimated in excess of £150,000. Instead the prisoners faced charges for the theft of a paltry £150 worth of miscellaneous articles from the 'down' train. Nevertheless, when the jury returned a verdict of 'guilty' against both prisoners, the judge showed no mercy in sentencing the pair to be 'transported for fifteen years'.

four

WINTER TALES

The Siege of Ladysmith

This story demonstrates the bravery displayed by the First Devon Regiment early in the New Year in 1900:

On New Year's Day 1900, a canon roared and British soldiers besieged by Boers at Ladysmith were astonished to see a shell explode in their midst releasing sweets. The Boers were showing off to crowds of sightseers who had celebrated the birth of the twentieth century by travelling out by special train from the Transvaal to witness their enemy's embarrassing predicament! A few days later, fifty Boer snipers gained possession of a ridge on Wagon Hill – the key position in the defence of Ladysmith. British troops surrounded them on three sides but were picked off at will by a hail of withering fire whenever they attempted to break cover. With the enemy concealed amongst the rocks it was decided that the only course of action available was to rush the enemy and attempt to rout the nest. During a terrible hailstorm, soldiers of the First Devon Regiment bravely charged out into the open and crossed a space of 125 metres with bayonets fixed to engage the Boers. They were led by Colonel Cecil Park, who later described the events:

> The men behaved most splendidly: every man went as straight and hard as he could... there wasn't the slightest sign of wavering... though as I ran I could see men falling like ninepins on both sides of me... then, at last... I saw the Boers jump up and fly down the hill for their lives and the position was ours...

However, the rocky ridge from which the Boers had been driven was not a straight line but curved at each end, exposing the British to a sudden heavy and damaging crossfire from each flank. A hero emerged to take a message to the Imperial Light Horse instructing them to open fire on the Boer positions. Lieutenant James Masterson of the First Devon Regiment received ten bullet wounds whilst undertaking this perilous mission and was awarded the Victoria Cross for conspicuous bravery. The citation published in the *London Gazette* read:

> During the action at Wagon Hill, on the 6th January 1900, Lieutenant Masterson commanded, with the greatest gallantry and dash, one of the three companies of his Regiment which charged a ridge held by the enemy and captured their position. The companies were then exposed to a most heavy and galling fire from the right and left front. Lieutenant Masterson undertook to give a message to the Imperial Light Horse, who were holding a ridge some hundred yards behind, to fire to the left front and endeavour to check the enemy's fire. In taking this message he crossed an open space of a hundred yards which was swept by a most heavy cross fire, and although badly wounded in both thighs managed to crawl in and deliver his message before falling exhausted into the Imperial Light Horse trench. His unselfish heroism was undoubtedly the means of saving several lives.

The rain and hail continued without let-up during the battle for Wagon Hill before the Boers' resistance was finally broken at nightfall. The British suffered 177 losses and 227 wounded during the day's fighting. Of the 189 officers and men from the First Devon Regiment who took part in the action, seventeen lost their lives and a further thirty-five were wounded. Half the survivors received bullet holes in their clothing and equipment. Lance Corporal Hole was one of those wounded during the battle and wrote home to his family in Torquay:

> I think that the Boers have got more than they bargained for this time, although they have slaughtered a lot of our men, are just as well armed as we are, and have good cattle to run about on. I never thought the Boers were so clever with their guns. I have seen some firing in my time, but this beats all.

Sir Redvers Buller VC.

The Commander-in-Chief of the British forces in South Africa was Lieutenant-General Sir Henry Redvers Buller, from Crediton, who twenty years earlier had himself been awarded the Victoria Cross for valour during the Zulu War. He sent a telegram to the gallant defenders, 'Congratulations for whole force on your brilliant defence and specially to Devon Regiment. Hope to meet you soon'. This last wish was accomplished on 28 February 1900 when Buller personally led the relief force into Ladysmith.

New Year's Morning Hymn

By Henry Francis Lyte from *Miscellaneous Poems* (1875). Whilst Vicar of All Saints Church, Brixham, the Reverend Henry Francis Lyte famously wrote the words to *Abide With Me* shortly before his death. In this hymn he looks forward to a peaceful existence in the afterlife:

Hail to another year,
The year that now begins!
All hail to Him who led us here
Through dangers and through sins!

Hail to another year!
Peace to the year that's past!
May this one at its close appear
Less worthless than the last!

BRIXHAM.

THE REVEREND
HENRY FRANCIS LYTE
Author of
"ABIDE WITH ME"

Abide with me; fast falls the eventide;
The darkness deepens; Lord, with me abide;
When other helpers fail and comforts flee,
Help of the helpless, O abide with me.

ALL SAINTS' CHURCH.　　　BERRY HEAD HOUSE

Henry Francis Lyte.

Hail to another year,
A year of peace and love!
Oh, may it prove a foretaste here
Of endless years above!

The Brooding Spirit of Rock House

This is the tale of Rudyard Kipling's unhappy experience living in Torquay:

The Nobel Prize for Literature, introduced in 1901, was not awarded to an English language writer until New Year's Eve 1907, when Rudyard Kipling (1865-1936) became its youngest recipient 'in consideration of the power of observation, originality of imagination, virility of ideas and remarkable talent for narration which characterize the creations of this world-famous author'.

The creator of literary classics including *The Jungle Book* and the *Just So* stories was born in India and named after Lake Rudyard in Staffordshire where his parents had first met. At the age of six, he and his three-year-old sister Trix were brought to England and deposited, without any explanation by their parents, at a boarding house in Southsea. Here they were raised and educated by a retired Naval officer and his wife until 1878 when Rudyard entered the United Services College at Westward Ho! Founded four years earlier, ostensibly to prepare boys for a military or naval career, this was never the intention for Kipling, as the college was chosen solely because his mother was a close friend of the headmaster, Cormwell Price.

Despite a miserable initiation period at the school, which he later recalled was 'primitive in its appointments, and our food would now raise a mutiny in Dartmoor [Prison]', the budding author flourished when the head realised 'I was irretrievably committed to the ink-pot', and Rudyard was appointed editor of the school magazine. A collection of his poems written at the college was published in India by his parents who believed in his potential. With fond memories of the establishment, dubbed by Kipling as 'the school before its time' he joyously returned to his family and embarked upon a journalistic career. He also drew inspiration from the land of his birth for his early literary successes. His output was stupendous and he became a marvellous storyteller, standing by the maxim that 'A word should fall in its place like a bell in a full chime'.

After travelling extensively, Kipling married American Caroline Baleister in 1892. The couple settled in her hometown of Brattleboro, Vermont, but their happiness was destroyed when Rudyard quarrelled with his brother-in-law, whom he had arrested for making violent threats – resulting in an embarrassing court appearance and damaging publicity. In the autumn of 1896, the Kiplings left this bitter episode behind them and moved to England. They rented Rock House at Maidencombe, Torquay, built on a cliff overlooking a small cove. The author described the villa as 'almost too good to be true' and waxed lyrical about the location. 'I look straight from my work table on to the decks of the fishing craft who come in to look after their lobster pots', he wrote. With the publication of his latest work, *The Seven Seas*, Kipling proudly accepted an invitation to spend several days with the Naval cadets based on the training ship *Britannia* at Dartmouth.

By Christmas, Kipling's enthusiasm for his new home declined as a sense of evil and brooding depression enveloped the household, which would later inspire his ghost story, *The House Surgeon*. He revealed a gathering blackness of mind and sorrow of the heart, 'It was the Feng-shui – the spirit of the house itself – that darkened the sunshine and fell upon us every time we entered, checking the very words on our lips.' He also disapproved of the posturing wealthy residents of the town. 'Torquay is such a place that I do desire acutely to upset by dancing through with nothing on but my spectacles.' For a time, he tried to fit in and took up the current craze for cycling. The gossip columnist of a local paper reported 'I saw Mr. Rudyard Kipling careering

Rudyard Kipling.

along the Tor Abbey sands on wheels one day last week.' The hobby ended when he and his wife shared pedalling duties on 'a tandem bicycle, whose double steering-bars made good dependence for continuous domestic quarrel'. The couple crashed off their 'Devil's toast rack' and walked home pushing the bike they dubbed 'Hell Spider'.

Before his brief sojourn on the English Riviera came to an abrupt end, Kipling fictionalised his school days. Local author Eden Phillpotts, best remembered for a cycle of eighteen novels set on Dartmoor, sent a copy of his latest book to Kipling, which immediately triggered an idea. Early in 1897, Kipling broached the subject with his editor, 'The notion of writing a Devonshire tale is new to me but, now I come to think of it, I was educated at Westward Ho! nigh Bideford and for six puppy years talked vernacular with the natives whose apples I stole. What will E.P. give to buy me off?' The result was *Stalky & Co.* based on the adventures of himself and his two closest friends at United Services College. His former headmaster, Cormwell Price, spent some time in Torquay hearing passages from the new book read to him by the excited author. Another rare happy moment occurred at Rock House when Caroline learned she was expecting the couple's third child. The Kiplings immediately executed 'our flight from Torquay' in May 1897 and sought refuge with relatives near Brighton. John Kipling, the son conceived in Torquay was doomed to die in action during the First World War. His father had to live with the guilt of his son's fate after 'pulling strings' to arrange for his enlistment after he had been rejected on medical grounds with extremely poor eyesight. Little wonder that when Rudyard revisited his former home shortly before his own death, the writer detected 'the same brooding Spirit of deep, deep Despondency within the open lit rooms'.

The Sporting Parson

Born in Dartmouth, the Reverend Jack Russell (1795-1883) was a hunting clergyman who bred the line of fox terriers that now bear his name. In this extract, his biographer E.W.L. Davies recounts how the septuagenarian rector of Swimbridge and Iddesleigh missed a Boxing Day meet for the first time soon after being introduced to the Prince and Princess of Wales in 1873:

The Reverend Jack Russell.

That the Prince and Princess were not unfavourably impressed with their west-country guest, on his first flying visit may be inferred from the circumstance that, shortly before his departure, the Prince sent [his equerry] Colonel Ellis to invite him again to Sandringham for the approaching Christmas week: 'And, as we hope to hear him preach', said the Prince, 'tell him to put a sermon in his pocket before he leaves home' …

No wonder, too, if Russell felt somewhat stirred by the coming event; nor, if, remembering the seventy-eight winters of his life, he might have wished for the magic cauldron of Media to restore him again to the vigour of his youth, and bring back, at least for one night, that 'freshness of the morning' which, with 'her clouds and her tears' the poet tells is 'worth evening's best light'.

Tally ho!

That would certainly have been his first wish had he
foreseen the honour that awaited him at the forthcoming
ball. On that night, a little before the clock struck twelve,
and a few minutes before the old year had passed away
for ever, Russell received the intimation that the Princess
was about to favour him with her hand and welcome the
incoming year by taking him for her partner. ...

It was whispered about by that little bird, to which, from
our earliest years, we have all been indebted for so much
authentic information, that Russell on hearing the tower
clock announce the birth of the new year, turned to his
fair partner and said, 'Now I can say what no man else can
ever say again'.

'And what may that be?' inquired the Princess with an
interested look.

'That I've had the honour of dancing out the old year and dancing in the new with Your Royal Highness'.

'Quite true', replied the Princess; 'no one else can say that but yourself'.

The Fox

Reynard comes off best in this traditional tale published by Sabine Baring-Gould in *Songs of the West* (1905):

The fox went out one winter night,
And prayed the moon to give him light,
For he'd many a mile to go that night,
Before he reached his den, O!
Den, O! Den, O!
For he'd many a mile to go that night,
Before he reached his den, O!

At last he came to a farmer's yard,
Where ducks and geese were all afear'd,
'The best of you all shall grease my beard,
Before I leave the town, O!
Town, O! Town, O!
The best of you all shall grease my beard,
Before I leave the town, O!'

He took the grey goose by the neck,
He laid a duck across his back,
And heeded not their quack! quack! quack!

The legs of all dangling down, O!
Down, O! Down, O!
And heeded not their quack! quack! quack!
The legs of all dangling down, O!

The old mother Slipper Slopper jump'd out of bed
And out of the window she po'd her head,
Crying 'Oh! John, John! The grey goose is dead,
And the fox is over the down, O!
Down, O! Down, O!'
Crying 'Oh! John, John! The grey goose is dead,
And the fox is over the down, O!'

Then John got up to the top o' the hill,
And blew his horn loud and shrill,
'Blow on' said Reynard, 'your music still,
Whilst I trot home to my den, O!
Den, O! Den, O!
'Blow on' said Reynard, 'your music still,
Whilst I trot home to my den, O!'

At last he came to his cosy den,
Where sat his young ones, nine or ten,
Quoth they, 'Daddy, you must go there again,
For sure 'tis a lucky town, O!
Town, O! Town, O!'
Quoth they, 'Daddy, you must go there again,
For sure 'tis a lucky town, O!'

The fox and his wife without any strife,
They cut up the goose without fork or knife,
And said, 'twas the best they had eat in their life,
And the young ones pick'd the bones, O!
Bones, O! Bones, O!
And said, 'twas the best they had eat in their life,
And the young ones pick'd the bones, O!

The Madness of Kisses

This story reveals how the spectacular fall from grace of a famous writer began in Torquay:

Literary genius Oscar Wilde (1854-1900) was at the height of his fame when he spent Christmas 1892 with his family in Torquay. He leased Babbacombe Cliff from the owner, Lady Mount-Temple, a distant cousin and confidante of Oscar's wife, Constance. Her mansion was designed by John Ruskin, Wilde's former lecturer on Florentine art at Oxford University. William Morris, who named all the bedrooms after flowers, created the interior décor. Oscar worked in the most artistic room in the house 'Wonderland', which was agreeable to Oscar's aesthetic tastes, for adorning the walls were paintings by Pre-Raphaelite artists Burne-Jones and Rossetti. Wilde also relaxed by swimming and sailing with his two sons off Babbacombe Beach. He wrote to Lady Mount-Temple whilst she was wintering abroad, 'I find the peace and beauty here so good for troubled nerves, and so suggestive for new work'.

During his stay, Oscar completed the play *A Woman of No Importance* and made arrangements to publish a limited edition of *Salome*, which had been banned from the stage by the Lord Chancellor because it depicted Biblical characters. In February 1893, he sent a copy to distinguished literary critic and Torquay resident, Edmund Gosse, 'Accept it as a slight tribute of my admiration of your own delicate use of the English'. Earlier, Wilde had supervised rehearsals of an amateur production of *Lady Windermere's Fan* directed by the Mayoress, Mrs Splatt, which opened in January 1893 at Torquay's Theatre Royal. He also granted an interview to local history author and solicitor Percy Almy that appeared in the magazine *The Theatre*. Amongst the topics they discussed were the merits of famous poets; Keats was the absolute 'favourite' of Wilde, Tennyson 'a supreme artist', Shelley 'a magnificent genius' though too 'ethereal'. Wilde had little regard for the work of Robert Browning, nor his wife Elizabeth, who before her marriage had spent three years recuperating from smallpox in Torquay. Almy observed that Wilde had 'an engaging charm' which would win him many disciples and interestingly, in view of the scandal that was about to engulf him, recorded the great man's thoughts on criminals, 'Never attempt to reform a man, men never repent'.

Oscar Wilde.

Early in February, Constance left to join friends in Florence. Immediately, Oscar was joined by his close friend Lord Alfred 'Bosie' Douglas, accompanied by his tutor who wrote of Wilde whilst staying in Babbacombe, 'I think him perfectly delightful with the firmest conviction that his morals are detestable'. Two years later, the relationship between Wilde and Bosie was to incite the boy's father, the Marquess of Queensbury, into denouncing Wilde as a 'sodomite'. Oscar responded by bringing an ill-advised libel case against Queensbury in April 1895. Produced in evidence was a damning letter written at Babbacombe Cliff, where Wilde had responded to a poem that Douglas had sent him:

> My boy, Your sonnet is quite lovely, and it is a marvel that those red rose-leaf lips of yours should have been made no less for music of song than for madness of kisses. Your slim gilt soul walks between passion and poetry. I know Hyacinthus, whom Apollo loved so madly, was you in Greek days.

His case collapsed and Oscar immediately found himself facing criminal charges on twenty-five acts of gross indecency, allegedly committed with a number of youths.

Two trials were necessary to decide Oscar's fate when the jury failed to agree a verdict. During the first, Constance sought refuge from the press at Babbacombe Cliff with Lady Mount-Temple. Whilst there, she wrote a letter seeking guidance from a fortune teller, Mrs Robinson, 'What is to become of my husband who has so betrayed me and deceived me and ruined the lives of my darling boys?'

The lady had already given the answer two years earlier at a party after the London opening of *A Woman of No Importance*. Wilde was noticeably distressed when told that his right palm revealed that he would 'send himself into exile'. Indeed, after serving two years hard labour in Reading Gaol, Wilde fled to France, where in his own words he was soon 'dying beyond my means'. Loyal friends bore the cost of his funeral and one of them complained with unintended Wildean wit, 'Dying in Paris is really a very difficult and expensive luxury for a foreigner!'

The Robin

The nation's favourite winter visitor is celebrated in this poem by Woodhouse Lane from *Dartmoor and Other Poems* (1918):

Welcome! cheery little friend,
Bright and bold and merry,
What a pretty breast you have,
As red as any berry.

You are a trusting little bird
Few other birds are able
To brave the terrors of a room,
And hop upon our table.

From dawn to dusk you sing your song
In the bleakest weather,

And only stop to feed or fight,
Or preen a ruffled feather.

You seem to love the winter well,
The hoar-frost and the snow,
The shelter of the holly-tree,
The bunch of mistletoe.

You are the sprite of Christmas
A kind of fairy Puck,

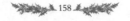

Who never lets a mortal pass
Without his share of luck.

So, here's a toast, my merry friend
'May you win a sprightly wife,
And own six baby robins,
And live a jolly life.'

Sinking Lower and Lower

This is the story of how a *Titanic* survivor fell foul of the
law some twenty years later:

At the wheel of the ill-fated *Titanic* at the moment of impact
with the deadly iceberg in April 1912 was quartermaster
Robert Hichens. Given charge of a lifeboat, Hichens took
the tiller and calmed his nerves by drinking liberally from a
bottle of spirit. Although the vessel was only carrying thirty
people – half of its capacity – he refused requests to search
for other survivors. As the stricken ship disappeared beneath
the waves, the cries and screams of people fighting for their
lives in the water could be plainly heard in the still night
air, but the seaman cruelly told the female occupants of the
lifeboat, 'It's no use; there's only a lot of stiffs out there'.

The inhumane attitude and over-reliance on alcohol
displayed by Hichens at this great moment of crisis was
to re-surface some twenty years later in Torquay. It was in
the same town, during the summer of 1906, that he had
met his future wife, Florence Mortimore. She was visiting

relatives in the resort, while he was on shore leave with the crew of a private yacht. Following a whirlwind courtship, the couple were married within a few months at the bride's parish church in the Dartmoor village of Manaton. Moving to Southampton, Hichens secured the prestigious appointment on the 'unsinkable' luxury liner. Following the terrible maritime disaster, Hichens returned to sea, serving with the Naval reserve during the First World War, after which he spent some time working with one of his brothers in South Africa. By 1930, he had relocated his family in Torquay and purchased a pleasure boat from businessman Harry Henley for the sum of £160, of which he paid a down payment of £100 with the remainder to be paid within two years. Unfortunately, tourists did not flock to take a trip around the bay on a vessel navigated by the man who sank the *Titanic*. The venture failed disastrously and Hichens was unable to repay the balance. Furthermore, he had borrowed the deposit from a Mr Squires, who seized the boat to settle the debt following a poor season's trading in 1931. The loss of his business caused Hichens to turn to drink and by the end of that year his wife had left him. For the next two years, her troubled husband scoured the country unable to find work and unreasonably chose to lay the blame for his predicament on the man who had sold him the boat. On his travels he acquired a revolver for £5 and journeyed to Torquay determined to kill Harry Henley.

Upon his arrival on 12 November 1933 he looked up an old friend, and told him, 'There will be two less in Torquay tonight. I've come down to do Henley and myself '. By early

Robert Hichens.

evening Hichens was drinking with another acquaintance who, hearing of the plan and shown the revolver, warned, 'Put it away. Don't be a fool. He isn't worth swinging for'. Worse the wear for drink, the gunman appeared to see sense and replied, 'I'll take your tip, I shan't give the hangman a job'. However, after closing time, having consumed rum in three public houses during the course of the evening, Hichens took a taxi to Harry Henley's home. Hearing a knock at the door, the unsuspecting victim came outside to see Hichens standing with both hands in his trouser pockets.

The sinking of the *Titanic*.

The unexpected caller demanded money, saying 'I am on the ground, I want you to pick me up'. Henley naturally replied, 'Why do you expect me to pick you up when you owe me £60 already?' Hichens gripped the revolver in his right-hand pocket and demanded 'Is that your last word?' To which his creditor replied, 'I wouldn't give you a penny piece if you were lying in the gutter'. Hichens then pulled out the pistol and with the words 'Take that' raised the weapon to the level of his target's head. Two gunshot explosions followed as Hichens fired the revolver at point blank range and very nearly succeeded in his desire to kill his former business associate.

Miraculously, one shot passed clean through the side of the victim's head without causing any internal damage. Henley felt a searing pain and subsequently lost a lot of blood but was fortunate not to suffer serious injury. The second shot went downwards and wide as Henley punched his assailant in the face giving him a bloody nose. Hichens fell to the floor, giving Henley the opportunity to run away and summon the police. Taken into custody in an intoxicated state, the prisoner enquired, 'Is he dead? I hope he is. He is a dirty rat, I would do it again if I had a chance, I intended to kill him and myself, too. He has taken my living away'.

Luckily for Hichens, the bullet that struck his victim had missed the brain by a fraction of an inch. Charged with attempted murder, the prisoner received an extraordinarily sympathetic hearing and a lenient sentence. Receiving an early Christmas present from the judge, he began five years imprisonment in December, after his defence counsel pleaded, with an unintended pun, that since his client's terrible ordeal on the *Titanic* he had been 'sinking lower and lower'.

Winter

By Beatrice Chase from *Gorse Blossoms from Dartmoor* (1916):

Breakfast to the robin's song
As the red sun rests his chin
Upon the moor's rim up along,
And stands there, looking in.

All day he plays a jovial game
With white King Frost and me,
His spears he throws with careful aim.
But Frost and he agree.

He blunts each spear lest it should break
The ice's gleaming fringe
That hangs right round the roof to make
The eaves an amber tinge.

He aims too at the fire of peat
That on the cobbit glows,
Pretending to eclipse its heat
With flames of gold and rose.

But Sun soon tires in winter-time
And goes to sleep his fill
Beneath a blanket of white rime
Upon the southern hill.

The old-gold curtain then we close
To bid the draughts decamp,
I blow the fire until it glows
And light the daffodil lamp.

Then comes on gold-embroidered cloth
The meal that I love most,
The cream with rim of bubble and froth,
Hot tea and buttered toast.

The full moon's cloudless light at last
Our artists souls entice
Outside to see her silver cast
Upon the fringe of ice.

The house has drawn the thatch right down
About her very eyes,
She sleeps beneath the hood of brown
Until the sun shall rise.

A Traveller's Tale

The wife of the Vicar of Tavistock, author Anna Eliza Bray, wrote this classic tale of suspense that was published in *The Borders of the Tamar and Tavy* (1879):

Well, then, once upon a time, as the old story-books say, there was a gentleman, who, mounted on a horse, (at the breaking up of a very hard and long frost, when the roads were only just beginning to be passable) set out in order to cross over Dartmoor. Now though the thaw had commenced, yet it had not melted the snow-heaps so much as expected: he got but slowly, and towards the close of day it began to freeze again. Shades of night were drawing all around him, and the mighty tors, which seemed to grow larger and taller as he paced forward, gradually became enveloped in vapour and in mist, and the traveller with his horse did not know what to do.

To reach Tavistock that night would be impossible, as a fresh snow-storm was fast falling in every direction, and would add to but another important impediment to the difficulties or dangers of his way. To stay out all night on the cold moor, without shelter or food, must be certain death, and where shelter was to be found somewhat puzzled the brains of our bewildered traveller. In this dilemma he still paced on, and at length he saw at a distance a certain dark object but partially covered with snow. As he drew nearer his heart revived; and his horse, which seemed to understand all the hopes and fears of his master, pricked up his ears and trotted, or rather slid, on a little faster. The discovery which has thus rejoiced the heart of man and beast was not only that of the dark object in question, but also of thick smoke, which rose like a stately column in the frosty air from its roof, and convinced him that what he now beheld must be a cottage.

He presently drew nigh and dismounted; and the rap that he gave with the butt-end of his whip upon the door, was answered by an old woman opening that portal of hope to him and his distresses. He entered and beheld a

Anna Eliza Bray.

sturdy peasant, that proved to be the old woman's son, and who sat smoking on his pipe over a cheerful and blazing peat fire. The traveller's wants were soon made known. An old outhouse with a litter of straw accommodated the horse, which, it is not unlikely, ate up his bed for the want of a better supper; but this is a point not sufficiently known to be asserted.

Of the affairs of the traveller I can speak with more certainty; and I can state, on the very best authority, that he felt very hungry and wanted a bed. Though there was but one besides the old woman's in the house, the son, who seemed to be a surly fellow, promised to give up his own bed for the convenience of the gentleman; adding that he would himself sleep that night in the old settle by the chimney-corner. The good dame busied herself in preparing such food as the house could afford for the stranger's supper; and at

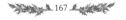

Winter warmers – Bagging a self-roasting pheasant!

length he retired to rest. Neither the room nor the bedding
were such as promised much comfort to a person accustomed to the luxuries of polished life; but as most things
derive their value from comparison, even so did these
mean lodgings, for they appeared to him to be possessed of
all that heart could desire, when he reflected how narrowly
he had escaped being perhaps frozen to death that night
on the bleak moor. Before going to rest he had observed
in the chamber a large oak-chest: it was somewhat curious
in form and ornament, and had the appearance of being
of very great antiquity. He noticed or made some remarks
upon it to the old woman, who had lighted up the stairs
in order to see that all things in his chamber might be as
comfortable as circumstances would admit for his repose.
There was something, he thought, shy and odd about the
manner of the woman when he observed the chest; and

after she was gone he had half a mind to take a peep into it. Had he been a daughter instead of a son of Eve he would most likely have done so; but as it was he forbore, and went to bed as fast as he could.

He felt cold and miserable; and who that does do can ever hope for a sound or refreshing sleep? His was neither the one nor the other, for the woman and the chest haunted him in his dreams; and a hollow sound, as if behind his bed's head, suddenly startled him out of his first sleep, when a circumstance occurred which, like the ominous voice to Macbeth, forbade him to sleep more. As he started up in bed, the first thing he saw was the old chest that had troubled him in his dreams. There it lay in the silvery silence of the moonlight, looking cold and white, and, connected with his dream, a provoking and even alarming object of his curiosity. And then he thought of the hollow sound which seemed to call him from his repose, and the old woman's odd manner when he had talked to her about the chest, and the reserve of her sturdy son, and, in short, the traveller's own imagination supplied a thousand subjects of terror; indeed so active did it become in these moments of alarm that it gave a tongue to the very silence of the night, and action even to the most inanimate things; for he looked and looked again, till he actually fancied the lid of the chest began to move slowly up before his eyes!

He could endure no more; but, starting from his bed, he rushed forward, grasped the lid with trembling hands, and raised it up at once. Who shall speak his feelings when he beheld what that fatal chest now disclosed? – a human corpse, stiff and cold, lay before his sight! So much was he overcome with the horror of his feelings, that it was with extreme difficulty he could once more reach the bed.

How he passed the rest of the night he scarcely remembered; but one thought, but one fear, possessed and agonised his whole soul. He was in the house of murderers! He was a devoted victim! There was no escape: for where, even if he left the chambers, at such an hour, in such a night, where should he find shelter, on the vast, frozen, and desolate moor? He had no arms, he had no means of flight; for if plunder and murder might be designed, he would not be suffered to pass out, when the young man (now, in his apprehension a common trafficker in the blood of the helpless) slept in the only room below, through which he must pass if he stirred from where he was.

To dwell on the thoughts and feelings of the traveller during what that night of terror would be an endless task; rather let me hasten to say that it was with the utmost thankfulness, and not without some surprise, that he found himself alive and undisturbed by any midnight assassin, when the sun once more arose and threw the cheerful light of day over the monotonous desolation of the moor. Under any circumstances, and even in the midst of a desert, there is pleasure and animation in the morning; like hope in the young heart, it renders all things beautiful. If such are its effects under ordinary circumstances, what must it have been to our traveller, who hailed the renewed day as an assurance of renewed safety to his own life? He determined, however, to hasten away; to pay liberally, but to avoid doing or saying anything to awaken suspicion.

On descending to the kitchen he found the old woman and her son busily employed in preparing no other fate for him than that of a good breakfast; and the son, who the night before was probably tired out with labour, had now lost what the gentleman fancied to have been a very surly humour. He gave his guest a country salutation, and hoping 'his honour' had found good rest, proceeded to recommend the breakfast in the true spirit, though in a rough phrase, of honest hospitality; particularly praising the broiled bacon, as 'mother was reckoned to have a curing hand at salting un in'.

Daylight civility, and broiled bacon, the traveller now found to be most excellent remedies against the terrors, both real and otherwise, of his own imagination. The fright had disturbed his nerves, but the keen air of those high regions, and the savoury smell of a fine smoking rasher,

Winter warmers – Coachman: 'I say sir, don't frighten the horses!'

were great restoratives. And as none but heroes of the old school of romance ever live without eating, I must say our gentleman gave convincing proofs that he understood very well the exercise of the knife and fork. Indeed so much did he feel re-assured and elevated by the total extinction of all his personal fears, that, just as the good woman was broiling him another rasher, he out with the secret of the chest, and let them know that he had been somewhat surprised by its contents; venturing to ask, in a friendly tone, for an explanation of so remarkable a circumstance.

'Bless your heart, your honour, tis nothing at all', said the young man, ''tis only fayther!'

'Father! your father!' cried the traveller, 'what do you mean?'

'Why you see, your honour', replied the peasant, 'the snaw being so thick, and making the roads so cledgey-like, when old fayther died, two weeks agon, we couldn't carry un to Tavistock to bury un; and so mother put un in the old box, and salted un in; mother's a fine hand at salting un in'.

Need a word more be said of the traveller and his breakfast; for so powerful was the association of ideas in a mind as imaginative as that of our gentleman, that he now looked with horror upon the smoking rasher, and fancied it nothing less than a slice of 'old fayther'. He got up, paid his lodgings, saddled his horse; and quitting the house, where surprise, terror, joy, and disgust had, by turns, so powerfully possessed him, he made his way through every impediment of snow and storm. And never could he afterwards be prevailed upon to touch bacon, since it always brought to mind the painful feelings and recollections connected with the adventures of 'salting un in'.

Childe the Hunter

Childe the Hunter is one of the oldest folk legends of Devon. Dating from the twelfth century, the story tells how John Childe, a wealthy landowner from Plymstock, was caught in a blizzard while hunting on Dartmoor. Completely lost and freezing cold, he killed and disembowelled his horse, then crawled inside the carcass to seek shelter. As the night wore on he realised he was dying of exposure and, dipping his finger in the horse's blood, wrote his will in the snow, leaving his estate to whichever church recovered his body and gave him a decent burial. When news of Childe's death spread, the abbeys of Tavistock and Buckfastleigh competed in an undignified race to claim the inheritance. When the friars of Tavistock got there first, the monks of Buckfast lay in wait by a bridge crossing the River Tavy, but their plan to steal the body was foiled when their rivals learned of the ambush and forded the river at a different spot. A granite cross known as Childe's Tomb was later erected to warn unwary travellers of the dangers they face when crossing the moor.

Come listen all, both great and small
To you a tale I'll tell,
What on this bleak and barren moor,
In ancient days befell,
It so befell, as I've heard tell,
There came the hunter Childe
All day he chased on heath and waste,
On Dart-a-moor so wild.

The winds did blow, then fell the snow,
He chased on Fox-tor mire;
He lost his way, and saw the day
And winter's sun expire
Cold blew the blast, the snow fell fast,
And darker grew the night;
He wandered high, he wandered low,
And nowhere saw a light.

In darkness blind he could not find
Where he escape might gain,
Long time he tried, no track espied,
His labours all in vain.
His knife he drew, his horse he slew,
As on the ground it lay:
He cut full deep, therein to creep,
And tarry till the day.

The winds did blow, fast fell the snow,
And darker grew the night,
Then well he wot, he hoped might not
Again to see the light.
So, with his finger dipped in blood,
He scrabbled on the stones,
'This is my will, God in fulfil,
And buried be my bones.

Whoe'er he be that findeth me
And brings me to a grave,
The lands that now to me belong,

In Plymstock he shall have.'
There was a cross erected then,
In memory of his name,
And there it stands, in wild waste lands,
To testify the same.

The Devil's Frying Pan

A naturally formed basin on Great Mis Tor where the souls of unrepentant sinners condemned to Hell were stir-fried and consumed by the Devil:

Exeter Stew With Devon Dumplings

To serve five or six persons remove all the fat from 2lbs of lean beef. Cut into eight or ten pieces and place in a stewing jar with two tablespoons of vinegar and place in a cool oven. To make a stock heat up 1½oz of dripping in a frying pan, fry two or three sliced onions with 1½oz of flour until brown. Add 1½ pints of water, bring to the boil then pour over the meat in the jar. Season with salt and pepper, cover closely and cook gently, either in the oven or on the stove for three hours. Make savoury dumplings with 4oz flour, 1½oz of finely chopped suet, one tablespoon of finely chopped parsley, ½ teaspoonful of powdered mixed herbs, 1 teaspoonful of salt, ¼ teaspoonful of baking powder, ½ salt spoonful of pepper. Place the ingredients in a bowl and add sufficient water to bind into a stiff mixture. Separate into twelve balls. About forty minutes before serving, bring the stew to boiling point, drop in the dumplings and simmer for forty minutes. To serve, pile the meat in the centre of a hot dish, strain the gravy over and arrange the balls neatly round the base.

Hot Tip
When making the stock use ¾ pint of water and ¾ pint of light ale.

Fruit Fritters
Apples – Peel and core and cut into rounds. Cover with sugar and leave to stand.
Bananas – Peel and scrape, split and cut in half again, squeeze a little lemon juice over them.
Oranges – Peel, scrape off the white skin, cut into rounds, remove pips, cover with sugar and leave to stand.
Pineapples – Drain the juice from a tin of pineapple slices, then add sugar to taste.

To cook, have the fat smoking hot in a deep frying pan. Dip the fruit in thick batter, made from 4oz of flour, one egg, ¼ pint of milk or water and a pinch of salt. Lift out the fritters and allow some of the batter to drip off, then drop gently into the fat. Fry until golden brown. Drain on soft paper. Place on a paper doyley on a hot dish and sprinkle with sugar.

Hot Tip
Serve the fritters with Devonshire whipped cream liberally flavoured with rum or brandy.

The Great Blizzard

There are many examples of the difficulties faced by rail users during the worst blizzard ever experienced in Devon:

The Great Blizzard of 1891 was the worst snowstorm experienced in England for fifty years. Freezing temperatures, unprecedented snowfalls and hurricane force gales took their toll with impassable roads, damaged property and pitiful tales of people found frozen to death in the snow. Yet despite the sufferings of the population at large, the press reserved most of its coverage for the railway system, which was paralysed for a week. The situation was summed up by the *Illustrated London News*:

> No such privations have ever been experienced in railway travel in this country within living memory… no one could have believed it possible that… people in England could be snowed up in trains, and in desperate peril for their lives.

The south-west region was hardest hit by the blizzard. Irate travellers gave critical interviews about long-delayed journeys in snowbound carriages, although their ordeals were minor compared to the lot of 1,200 Great Western Railway labourers ordered not to return to their homes until the line was cleared all the way from Bristol to Penzance. In conditions so cold that the snow froze on their clothes, encasing them in ice, they accomplished their arduous and dangerous mission with only one fatality that occurred on the Plymouth to Totnes line. Snowploughs working from opposite ends at Plympton and Kingsbridge gradually forced their way through 20ft drifts in which five trains were embedded. The two breakdown gangs met at Ivybridge and had just succeeded in hoisting an engine back on to the metals when a relief train from Plymouth came around a bend at 25mph and crashed into a stationary carriage of the snowed-up train. Two workmen were seriously injured in the collision and William Stentiford, a recently married Plymouth man, lost his life.

The London train due to arrive at Plymouth at 8.55 p.m. on Monday night came to grief at Brent, one of the most exposed towns on Dartmoor. The hotels were full with contractors' men engaged to lay a new railway line and the forty stranded passengers were forced to remain on the train or sleep in the station waiting room for several days. A disgruntled commercial traveller, Mr Stumbles, complained bitterly about the uncharitable treatment they had received from the tradesmen of Brent:

> The inns charged us double price for ordinary meals, and some establishments refused to supply us at all, probably thinking that a famine was impending. We returned to the station as best we could, through the great drifts of snow, and, with such provisions as we could buy, cooking such things as bloaters in the station waiting room. Our scanty supply, I must say, was most generously supplemented from the small stores which the railway officials, such as the signalman and others, had with them.

The stranded Princetown train.

The *Western Morning News*, which published this story, also discovered that inflation was rife amongst the hypocritical travellers. In fact, the value of their own newspaper had increased substantially during the short period that the passengers had been cut off from the world. A copy was taken to Brent by a policeman from Totnes who braved the elements and gave it to one of the beleaguered passengers. It was later revealed that the lucky recipient then turned down an offer of £2 for exclusive ownership from a fellow traveller and instead accepted 5s (25p) to allow him to read it for one hour.

Probably the most alarming incident experienced by passengers occurred on the normally short journey from Princetown to Plymouth on the Dartmoor branch line. Starting out at 6.20 p.m., the train struggled only as far as Peak Tor before pulling up with a jolt. The driver immediately alarmed the passengers by admitting, 'We ought not to have started'. The fireman sustained an injury to his leg when the engine pulled up but joined the driver and guard in an unsuccessful attempt to clear the line with shovels. The guard then set out to walk to Dousland for help. The falling snow blinded him and the drifts were so deep that he could not even follow the track. One hour later he gratefully returned to the relative safety of the train. The six male and two female passengers gathered in a composite carriage of one first class, one second-class and four third-class compartments where they were to spend the first of two uncomfortable nights. A passenger later described the appalling conditions:

> The snow beat in our compartment through closed doors, ventilators, and windows, so much, that in a few minutes I had two inches of snow on my umbrella. We stuffed paper,

Dartmoor ponies seek refuge at Princetown during a blizzard.

handkerchiefs, and cloth into every hole or crevice we could find, and this remedied matters a little.

Early next morning, driver Bulland set out in a raging snowstorm and against the odds reached Dousland. The GWR immediately despatched two men with simple fare of brandy, cocoa, bread and cake, which was delivered to the forlorn passengers at 3 p.m. They then spent an anxious time waiting for rescue as the wind howled and the temperatures remained bitterly cold. By now an elderly married couple were suffering from the effects of exposure. At 7 a.m. on Wednesday, the travellers awoke from a fitful sleep to find the weather had partially cleared and help was unexpectedly close at hand. The train, which by this time was almost completely covered in snow with drifts as high as the carriage, was discovered by Farmer Hilson of Horsford, who was out in his fields rescuing buried sheep. Unbelievably, his farmhouse was only 200 yards away from the train and he was astounded that he been totally unaware of their plight. Gratefully swapping the cold comfort of the carriage for the hearty hospitality of the farmhouse, the passengers were soon warming up and enjoying breakfast. A railway journey had become a test of survival and they began to wonder why the train was running at all considering the Princetown stationmaster's gloomy forecast when they had sought to buy tickets two days earlier, 'You can have them, but I cannot promise you will get there'.

Dartmoor Prison at Princetown had a reputation as being the most inhospitable place in which to serve time. Conditions were even worse during the blizzard and soon trouble was brewing as inmates were repeatedly fed rations of salted meat. After a week in which no fresh provisions could be delivered by train, resentment and insubordination grew to such a fever pitch that a warder was attacked and stabbed in the neck by a convict. The governor reported the worrying situation to the Home Secretary, who contacted the railway company requesting them to clear the line of snow as a matter of urgency. Fifty workmen were despatched on a train accompanied by a snowplough but the work had to abandoned near Yelverton station when they were faced with a 200 yard-long drift. Next day, eighty men set out and cut a path through the drift and made it as far as Dousland. Late in the evening of the third day of the operation, a special goods train with provisions from Plymouth finally made it to Princetown to alleviate the mood of the convicts. The most thankful people to see the train service resumed were those prisoners due for release who had been forced to accept their situation as 'boarders' until conditions improved.

The Months of the Year

From *Songs of the West* (1905):

> First comes January
> When the sun lies very low;
> I see in the farmer's yard
> The cattle feed on straw.
> The weather being so cold

While the snow lays on the ground
There will be another change of moon
Before the year comes round.

Next is February,
So early in the spring;
The farmer ploughs the fallows,
The rooks their nest begin.
The little lambs appearing
Now frisk in pretty play;
I think upon the increase,
And thank my God, today.

March it is the next month,
So cold and hard and drear;
Prepare we now for harvest,
By brewing of strong beer.
God grant that we who labour,
May see the reaping come;
And drink and dance and welcome,
The happy harvest home.

Next of months is April,
When early in the morn;
The cheery farmer soweth,
To right and left the corn.
The gallant team come after,
A-smoothing of the land;
May Heaven the farmer prosper,
Whate'er he takes in hand.

In May I go a'walking,
To hear the linnets sing;
The blackbird and the throstle,
A-praising God the King.
It cheers the heart to hear them,
To see the leaves unfold;
The meadows scattered over,
With buttercups of gold.

Full early in the morning,
Awakes the summer sun;
The month of June arriving,
The cold and night are done.
The cuckoo is a fine bird,
She whistles as she flies;
And as she whistles, cuckoo,
The bluer grow the skies.

Six months I have now named,
The seventh is July;
Come lads and lasses gather,
The scented hay to dry.
All full of mirth and gladness,
To turn it in the sun;
And never cease till daylight sets,
And all the work is done.

August brings the harvest,
The reapers now advance;
Against their shining sickles,

Dartmoor Prison.

The field stands little chance.
'Well done!' exclaims the farmer,
'This day is all men's friend;
We'll drink and feast in plenty,
When we the harvest end'.

By middle of September,
The rake is laid aside;
The horses wear the breeching,
Rich dressing to provide.
All things to do in season,
Me-thinks is just and right;
Now summer season's over,
The frosts begin at night.

October leads in winter,
The leaves begin to fall;
The trees will soon be naked,

No flowers left at all.
The frosts will bite them sharply,
The elm alone is green;
In orchard piles of apples red,
For cider press are seen.

The eleventh month, November,
The nights are cold and long;
By day we're felling timber,
And spend the night in song.
In cosy chimney corner,
We take our toast and ale;
And kiss and tease the maidens,
Or tell a merry tale.

Then comes dark December,
The last of months in turn;
With holly, box, and laurel,
We house and church adorn.
So now, to end my story,
I wish you all good cheer,
A merry happy Christmas,
A prosperous New Year.

BIBLIOGRAPHY
& SOURCES

The Spirit of Christmas Past
Dickens in Devon:
Holgate, Mike. 'The Spirit of Christmas', *Devon Life*, December 1998

A Christmas Carol:
Dickens, Charles. *The Posthumous Papers of the Pickwick Club*, London, Chapman and Hall, 1837

Christmas Day:
Kingsley, Charles. *Poems*, London, Macmillan & Co., 1897

Christmas Morning in Exeter Cathedral:
Illustrated London News, 25 December 1852

Lux Mundi:
Torquay Times Christmas Issue, 25 December 1931

Hymn on the Nativity:
Colling, Mary Maria. *Fables and other pieces in verse*, London, Longman, Rees, Orme, Brown & Green 1831

The Bell of Bethlehem:
Torquay Times Christmas Issue, 25 December 1938

Christmas Bells:
Capern, Edward. *Poems by Edward Capern, rural postman of Bideford, Devon*,
    London, David Bogue, 1856

The Christmas Bazaar:
Devon Weekly Times, 24 December 1875

The Christmas Tree:
Phillpotts, Eden. *A Hundred Lyrics*, London, Ernest Benn, 1930

The First Christmas Card:
John Calcott Horsley and Orestone, Torbay Civic Society, 1988
www.victoriana.com

Old Father Christmas:
Burington, E.H. *Trewmans Exeter Flying Post*, 26 December 1850

The Magic Log:
Emmett, Eugenie. *Torquay Times Christmas Number*, 25 December 1938

God Sends Meat but the Devil Sends Cooks:
Beeton, Isabella (ed). *Beeton's Book of Household Management*, London, S.O.
    Beeton, 1859
Doyle, Arthur Conan. *A Duet, with an Occasional Chorus*, London, G.
    Richards, 1899
www.legendarydartmoor.co.uk

The Devil's Kitchen:
Beeton, Isabella. *Beeton's Cookery*, London, Ward Locke, 1910
Radiation Cookery Book, London, Radiation Ltd, 1927
www.legendarydartmoor.co.uk

The Adventure of the Christmas Pudding:
Christie, Agatha. *An Autobiography*, London, William Collins Sons & Co., 1977
Babbage, Charles. *Passages From the Life of a Philosopher*, London,
    Longman & Co., 1864

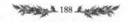

Scott, Robert Falcon, *The Voyage of the 'Discovery'*, London, Smith, Elder & Co., 1905

Gosse, Edmund, *Father and Son: a study of two temperaments*, London, Heinemann, 1907

The Prize Turkey:
Western Daily Mercury, 27 December 1892

Heaven in Devon:
Chase, Beatrice. *Torquay Times Christmas Issue*, 25 December 1927

Christmas Decorations:
Herrick, Robert. *Hesperides or the works both humane and divine of Robert Herrick Esq*, London, John Williams & Francis Eglesfield, 1648

The Holy Ghost of Lapford:
Holgate, Mike. 'The Holy Ghost of Lapford', *Devon Life*, December 2001

Yuletide Tipples & Spirits

A Devonshire Ghost Story:
Seage, G. *Devon Weekly Times*, 24 December 1896

The Wassailing:
A Dish of Apples, London, Hodder & Stoughton, 1921

Devonshire Cider:
Williamson, Anne. *Henry William Williamson* in Oxford *Dictionary of National Biography*, Oxford, Oxford University Press, 2004
Williamson, Henry. *The Village Book*, London, Jonathan Cape, 1930

The Merry Carol Singers:
Baring-Gould, Sabine. *Further Reminiscences 1864-1894*, London, John Lane, The Bodley Head, 1925

The Drunken Maidens:
Baring-Gould, Sabine; Sheppard, H. F; Bussell, F.W: Sharp, Cecil J. (eds). *Songs of the West*, London, Methuen & Co., 1905

The Ghost of the Little Giant:
Holgate, Mike. 'The Little Giant', *Devon Life*, April 2002

I Wish You Merry Christmas:
Matthews, F.W. *Tales of the Blackdown Borderland*, London, Somerset Folk
    Books, 1923

The Devil's Punchbowl:
Beeton, Isabella. *Beeton's Cookery*, London, Ward Locke, 1910
Radiation Cookery Book, London, Radiation Ltd, 1927
www.legendarydartmoor.co.uk

A Yankee at King Arthur's Court:
Holgate, Mike. 'Plymouth's Political Pioneer', *Young At Heart*, November
    1997

Sir John Barleycorn:
Baring-Gould, Sabine; Sheppard, H. F; Bussell, F.W; Sharp, Cecil J. (eds).
    Songs of the West, London, Methuen & Co., 1905

Christmas Time – Mystery and Crime

Christmas 'Time' on Dartmoor:
Holgate, Mike. 'Christmas "Time" on Dartmoor', *Devon Life*, December
    2006

The Christmas Sale:
Whitfield, H.F. *Plymouth and Devonport, in Times of War and Peace*,
    Plymouth, E. Chapple 1900

The Man They Could Not Hang:
Holgate, Mike. 'And Thereby Hangs a Tale', *Devon Life*, December 2007

A Living Hell:
Lee, John. *The Man They Could Not Hang*, London, C. Arthur Pearson,
    1908

Devonshire Cream:
Hawker, J.M. *Transactions of the Devonshire Association*, Dawlish, 1881

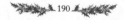

Jack the Ripper in Devon:
Holgate, Mike. *Jack the Ripper: The Celebrity Suspects*, Stroud, The History
    Press, 2008

The Kenton Ghost:
Tickler. *Devon Weekly Times*, 23 December 1864

A Twist in the Plot:
Holgate, Mike. 'A Twist in the Plot', *Devon Life*, December 2001

A Christmas Carol:
Derwent and Susan Coleridge (eds). *The Poems of Samuel Taylor Coleridge*,
    London, Edward Moxon, 1852

The Great Pearl Mystery:
British Medical Journal
Illustrated London News
Illustrated Police News
Torquay Times
Western Daily Mercury

The Great Western Train Robbery:
Holgate, Mike. 'Crime on the Line', *Devon Life*, January 2006

Winter Tales

The Siege of Ladysmith:
Holgate, Mike. 'The Siege of Ladysmith', *Devon Life*, December 1999

New Year's Morning Hymn:
Lyte, by Henry Francis. *Miscellaneous Poems*, London, Rivingtons, 1875

The Brooding Spirit of Rock House:
Holgate, Mike. 'Stalky & Co in Westward Ho!', *Devon Life*, December
    2007

The Sporting Parson:
The Out-of-Door Life of the Rev. John Russell, London, Chatto & Windus,
    1878

The Fox:
Baring-Gould, Sabine; Sheppard, H. F; Bussell, F.W: Sharp, Cecil J. (eds).
    Songs of the West, London, Methuen & Co., 1905

The Madness of Kisses:
Holgate, Mike. 'Wilde About Babbacombe', *Devon Life*, January 2001

The Robin:
Lane, Woodhouse. *Dartmoor and Other Poems*, Bristol, 1918

Sinking Lower and Lower:
Holgate, Mike. *Murder & Crime: Devon*, Gloucester, Tempus Publishing,
    2007

Winter:
Chase, Beatrice. *Gorse Blossoms from Dartmoor*, London, Longman, 1916

A Traveller's Tale:
Bray, Anne Eliza Bray. *The Borders of the Tamar and Tavy*, London, W. Kent
    & Co., 1879

Childe the Hunter:
Baring-Gould, Sabine; Sheppard, H. F; Bussell, F.W, Sharp, Cecil J. (eds).
    Songs of the West, London, Methuen & Co., 1905

The Devil's Frying Pan:
Beeton, Isabella. *Beeton's Cookery*, London, Ward Locke, 1910
Radiation Cookery Book, London, Radiation Ltd, 1927
www.legendarydartmoor.co.uk

The Great Blizzard:
Holgate, Mike. *Murder & Mystery on the Great Western Railway*, Tiverton,
    Halsgrove Publishing, 2006

The Months of the Year:
Baring-Gould, Sabine; Sheppard, H.F; Bussell, F.W, Sharp, Cecil J. (eds)
    Songs of the West, London, Methuen & Co., 1905